KB173799

First Step in
English Discussion

2
Student Book

IaM books

Preface

First Step in English Discussion series is a basic discussion book for beginner learners. There are 12 units in series and each unit is about a different point of English speaking which is very helpful for an English-learner students. With the various exercises, interesting photos and illustrations, students will enjoy all the skills (reading, writing, listening, and speaking) and really can communicate in English, even from the beginning. This book encourages students to speak and write English accurately and fluently by providing them with a solid understanding of English language.

This book uses a simple but systematic approach (Getting Ready, Reading, Dialogue, Supper Discussion, and Language Focus) to help young learners master English speaking skills.

This series aims to motivate young learners to develop their speaking skills that will help students throughout their lives through various creative tasks such as Super Discussion and various levels of challenging questions.

First Step in English Discussion series is a useful supplement to any English language course and is suitable for both classroom teaching and self-study. The series focuses on the strong oral skills development that students need to know for basic interpersonal communication skills.

I hope many students will build language and communication skills with this *First Step in English Discussion series*. At the same time, I wish teachers will use *First Step in English Discussion series* as the most appropriate tool for teaching English as a second language.

I am convinced that through this *First Step in English Discussion series*, a lot of students will definitely have the opportunity to improve and develop their English speaking skills and abilities.

Thanks and good luck,
Lucifer EX

Contents

About This Book

step 1. Getting Ready
- This task prepares students by previewing the unit's language and ideas.
- Represent short and practical dialogs
- Key vocabulary is presented in various formats.
- The accompanying short questions ensure that students understand the topic of the Unit with colorful photos.

step 2. Reading
- This section contains a reading passage about the main topic.
- Present key vocabulary
- Develop reading skills

step 3. Building vocabulary
- Students learn vocabulary from the Reading passage.
- This vocabulary is used throughout the reading passage, so that students gradually become familiar with it.

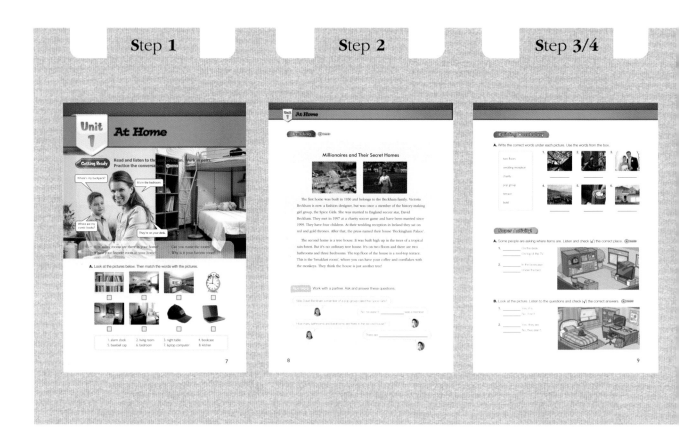

step 4. **Super Activity!**

• Develop listening skills through targeted tasks and visual cues

step 5. **Dialog**

• Develop listening skills
• The listening task focuses on understanding the topic and related issues of the dialogue, and then focuses on detail and interpretation.

step 6. **Supper Discussion!**

• Students discuss the topic and related issues.

step 7. **Super Speaking**

• Super Speaking offers students rich opportunities to broaden and improve their speaking skills. Students work in pairs or groups and perform a variety of real-life tasks, progressing smoothly from controlled to free practice. By doing so, the amount of time students speak is increased significantly and cooperation among students is encouraged. In addition, pair and group work help students lessen their communicative stress because it is easier for them to communicate with their peers rather than their teachers.

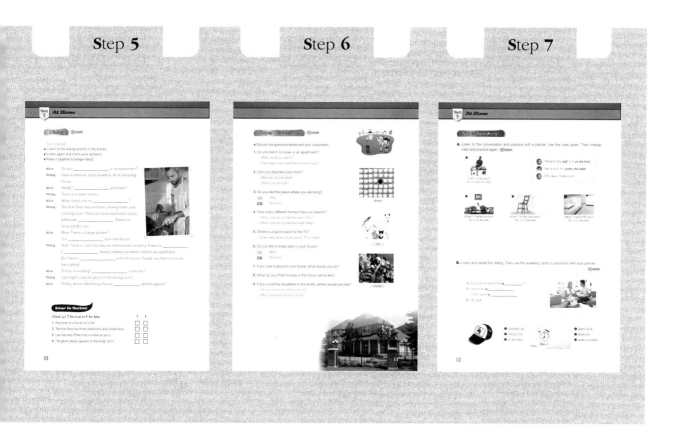

About This Book

step 8. Learn & Practice

- Vivid photos and illustrations stimulate students' interest and help them understand the meaning and use of grammar. Clear and easy-to-read grammar charts present the grammar structure. The accompanying examples ensure that students understand the grammar point with colorful photos.

step 9. Exercise

- Each Learn & Practice provides various basic exercises and opportunities to practice both the forms and the uses of the grammar structure.

step 10. Super Speaking

- Super Speaking offers students rich opportunities to apply newly learned grammar to speaking activities. This section will help students to develop speaking skills. Students work in pairs or groups and perform a variety of real-life tasks, progressing smoothly from controlled to free practice.

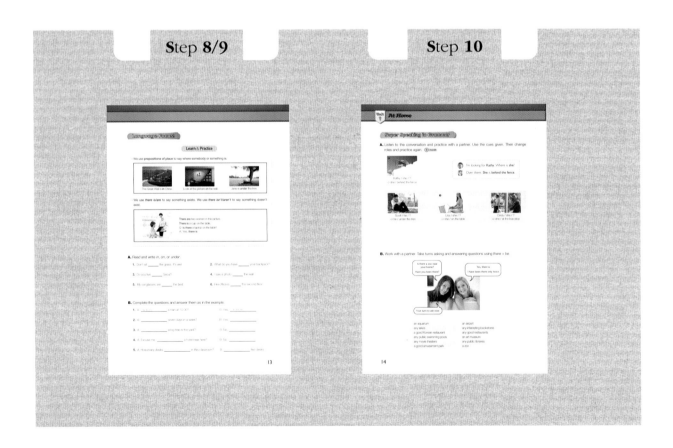

Step 8/9   Step 10

Read and listen to the conversation. Work in pairs. Practice the conversation. Track 1

Where's my backpack?

It's in the bedroom.

Where are my comic books?

They're on your desk.

- How many rooms are there in your home?
- What's your favorite room in your home?
- Can you name the rooms?
- Why is it your favorite room?

A. Look at the pictures below. Then match the words with the pictures.

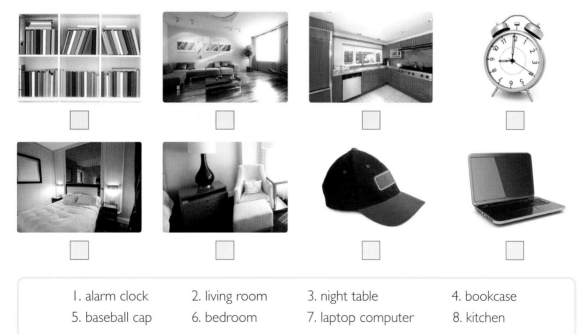

| 1. alarm clock | 2. living room | 3. night table | 4. bookcase |
| 5. baseball cap | 6. bedroom | 7. laptop computer | 8. kitchen |

Reading Track 2

Millionaires and Their Secret Homes

The first home was built in 1930 and belongs to the Beckham family. Victoria Beckham is now a fashion designer, but was once a member of the history-making girl group, the Spice Girls. She was married to England soccer star, David Beckham. They met in 1997 at a charity soccer game and have been married since 1999. They have four children. At their wedding reception in Ireland they sat on red and gold thrones. After that, the press named their house 'Beckingham Palace'.

The second home is a tree house. It was built high up in the trees of a tropical rain forest. But it's no ordinary tree house. It's on two floors and there are two bathrooms and three bedrooms. The top floor of the house is a roof-top terrace. This is the 'breakfast room', where you can have your coffee and cornflakes with the monkeys. They think the house is just another tree!

Pair Work Work with a partner. Ask and answer these questions.

Was David Beckham a member of a pop group called the Spice Girls?

No, he wasn't. _____ was a member.

How many bathrooms and bedrooms are there in the second house?

There are _____.

Building Vocabulary

A. Write the correct words under each picture. Use the words from the box.

two floors

wedding reception

charity

pop group

terrace

build

1.

_____

2.

_____

3.

_____

4.

_____

5.

_____

6.

_____

Super Activity!

A. Some people are asking where items are. Listen and check (✓) the correct place. 🔘 Track 3

1. _____ On the desk

   _____ On top of the TV

2. _____ In the bookcase

   _____ Under the bed

B. Look at the picture. Listen to the questions and check (✓) the correct answers. 🔘 Track 4

1. _____ Yes, it is.

   _____ No, it isn't.

2. _____ Yes, they are.

   _____ No, they aren't.

Dialog Track 5

Two students:
- Listen to the dialog and fill in the blanks.
- Listen again and check your answers.
- Read it together (change roles).

Alice   Do you _____ or an apartment?

Phillip   I live in a house. I just moved in. It's a really big house.

Alice   Really? _____ are there?

Phillip   There are seven rooms.

Alice   What rooms are on _____?

Phillip   The first floor has a kitchen, a living room, and a dining room. There are three bedrooms and a bathroom _____. There's a large garden, too.

Alice   Wow! There's a large garden?

You _____ your new house.

Phillip   Yeah. I love it. Last Saturday we had a barbecue party. It was so _____.

I _____ having a barbecue when I lived in an apartment.

But there's _____ with the house. People say that our house has a ghost.

Alice   Phillip, no kidding! _____ scare me?

Phillip   Last night I saw the ghost in the dining room.

Alice   Phillip, do you like living a house _____ ghosts appear?

Answer the Questions

Check (√) T for true or F for false   T   F

1. Alice lives in a house on a hill. ☐ ☐

2. The first floor has three bedrooms and a bathroom. ☐ ☐

3. Last Saturday Phillip had a barbecue party. ☐ ☐

4. The ghost always appears in the living room. ☐ ☐

● Discuss the questions below with your classmates.

1. Do you live in a house or an apartment?
  ▶ What city do you live in?
  ▶ How many rooms are there in your house?

2. Can you describe your room?
  ▶ What are on your desk?
  ▶ What is on the wall?

different

3. Do you like the place where you are living?
  Yes! .. Why?
  No! .. Why not?

4. How many different homes have you lived in?
  ▶ Which one did you like the best? Why?
  ▶ Which one did you like the least? Why?

pets

5. Where is a good place for the TV?
  ▶ How many times do you watch TV in a day?

6. Do you like to keep pets in your house?
  Yes! .. Why?
  No! .. Why not?

7. If you saw a ghost in your home, what would you do?

8. What do you think houses in the future will be like?

9. If you could live anywhere in the world, where would you live?
  ▶ Which country would you choose?
  ▶ Why? Tell everyone your choice.

choose

Super Speaking!

A. Listen to the conversation and practice with a partner. Use the cues given. Then change roles and practice again. ⊙ Track 7

❶

ball? / on the bed?
No ⇨ under the table

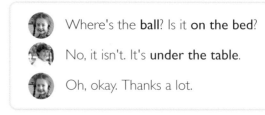

Where's the **ball**? Is it **on the bed**?

No, it isn't. It's **under the table**.

Oh, okay. Thanks a lot.

❷

picture? / behind the door
No ⇨ on the wall

❸

book? / on the night table?
No ⇨ on the chair

④

pillow? / next to the door
No ⇨ on the sofa

B. Listen and repeat the dialog. Then use the speaking cards to practice it with your partner.

⊙ Track 8

A: Do you know where the ❶ __magazine__ is?

B: Look in the ❷ ____living room____ .

  I think I saw it ❸ ____under the sofa____ .

B: Oh, yeah.

❶ baseball cap
❷ dining room
❸ on the table

❶ alarm clock
❷ bedroom
❸ under your bed

Learn & Practice

- We use **prepositions of place** to say where somebody or something is.

The Great Wall is **in** China.

Look at the picture **on** the wall.

Jane is **under** the tree.

- We use *there is/are* to say something exists. We use *there isn't/aren't* to say something doesn't exist.

There are two women in this picture.
There is a cup on the table.
Q: **Is there** a laptop on the table?
A: Yes, **there is**.

A. Read and write *in*, *on*, or *under*.

1. Don't sit _____ the grass. It's wet.

2. What do you have _____ your backpack?

3. Do you live _____ Seoul?

4. I saw a photo _____ the wall.

5. My sunglasses are _____ the bed.

6. Her office is _____ the second floor

B. Complete the questions and answer them.

1. A: _Is there_____ a train at 10:00?   B: Yes, __there is_____.

2. A: _____ seven days in a week?   B: Yes, _____.

3. A: _____ a big tree in the yard?   B: No, _____.

4. A: Excuse me, _____ a hotel near here?   B: No, _____.

5. A: How many desks _____ in this classroom?   B: _____ two desks.

Super Speaking in Grammar

A. Listen to the conversation and practice with a partner. Use the cues given. Then change roles and practice again. Track **9**

Kathy / she / ?
⇨ she / behind the fence

> I'm looking for **Kathy**. Where is **she**?
>
> Over there. **She** is **behind the fence**.

Scott / he / ?
⇨ he / under the tree

Lisa / she / ?
⇨ she / on the table

Cindy / she / ?
⇨ she / at the bus stop

B. Work with a partner. Take turns asking and answering questions using *there + be*.

Is there a zoo near your home?

Have you been there?

Yes, there is.

I have been there only twice.

Your turn to ask now.

an aquarium	an airport
any lakes	any interesting bookstores
a good Korean restaurant	any good restaurants
any public swimming pools	an art museum
any movie theaters	any public libraries
a good amusement park	a zoo

Past Events

Read and listen to the conversation. Work in pairs. Practice the conversation. ⊙ Track 10

How was your weekend, Jane?

It was pretty good.

What did you do?

Well, on Saturday morning I played soccer with my dad.

How was your weekend?   What kinds of activities did you do on the weekend?

A. Look at the pictures below. Then match the correct phrases to each picture.

1. went for a bicycle ride   2. stayed and watched TV   3. did my homework   4. played soccer
5. met some friends   6. went to the movies   7. cleaned my room   8. went to the beach

15

Reading Track 11

How Was Your Weekend?

Hello! My name's Peter. I'm from Canada. On Saturday morning I got up late. I ate breakfast and read a magazine. In the afternoon I went to the Museum of Art History with my younger sister. As soon as I entered the museum, I found there were so many wonderful pictures. Among them, the paintings by Rubens were very impressive. After we had lunch, we went to the central park. A few small boys and girls were playing in the park. We saw them throwing paper on the grass and throwing bottles in the pond. We went to them and said. "Good boys and girls, don't throw paper on the grass and bottles in the pond!" They were very sorry. They quickly put the paper and bottles in a big garbage can.

Hello! I'm Cindy. Last weekend was fantastic! My father and I decided to go to Rome to visit Aunt Sophie, Uncle Daniel and my cousins Mark and Tina. We traveled by plane on Friday afternoon and arrived at the airport at seven o'clock in the evening. A taxi drove us from the airport to my uncle and aunt's house. We had a delicious dinner and went to bed early because we were tired. On Saturday morning we visited the city, saw beautiful places and incredible monuments. It was wonderful. I was sorry that mom couldn't come with us. She had to practice for the competition and didn't have time to tour Rome with us. In the afternoon we bought some souvenirs and ate ice creams. Then my cousins and I went to the "Time Elevator" where we learned about the history of Rome, while watching a 3D film with lots of special effects. After I had dinner, I wrote an e-mail to my friends in England and read some comic books before going to sleep. On Sunday we had lunch in a restaurant and then we went back to England. It was a really nice weekend!

enter

throw

souvenirs

competition

A. What did these people do last weekend? Listen and circle the correct answer.  ◉ Track 12

1. He _____ .

    a. went to the movies with his friends

    b. went to Jeju island with his family

2. She _____ .

    a. went to a party

    b. watched an adventure movie on TV

Pair Work   What did you do last weekend? Ask your partner.

B. Listen to the conversations and write the numbers in the correct pictures. ◉ Track 13

1.

□

2.

□

3.

□

C. Listen and write T for true, F for false. ◉ Track 14

1. Scott stayed home and watched TV on Saturday night.

    ⇨ _____

2. Scott and Jessica had to study for their exams during the weekend.

    ⇨ _____

3. Scott and Jessica ate a nice dinner and went to a movie.

    ⇨ _____

4. Jessica went to a jazz concert with her grandfather.

    ⇨ _____

Dialog Track 15

Two students:
- Listen to the dialog and fill in the blanks.
- Listen again and check your answers.
- Read it together (change roles).

Sarah	How was your _____?
Ron	_____. I just went to the movies.
Sarah	What did you watch?
Ron	I _____ the latest action movie.
Sarah	Oh, I really want to see that, too!
Ron	Well, I don't really recommend it.
Sarah	Oh yeah? _____?
Ron	It fell short of my expectations. The story was _____.
Sarah	I see. How were the actors' performances?
Ron	They were so so. _____ on the weekend?
Sarah	Well, on Saturday morning I played tennis, on Saturday afternoon I went to the beach, and on Saturday night I went to baseball game.
Ron	Cool.
Sarah	Then, on Sunday morning, I _____ and studied for the math test. On Sunday afternoon, I played soccer and _____. On Sunday night, I had _____.
Ron	How was it?
Sarah	He was a nice guy but there was no _____ between us.

Weekend Activities Track 16

People have many different things to do at weekends. Some may spend time at the beach. Others could take a whole day to visit friends or go on a picnic. What about you? What do you do on your weekends? "What did you do last weekend?" Ask thousands of people that question and you get an average answer - an idea of what everybody does on the weekend. So, what did the average person do last weekend? Well, 85 percent of the people went to a movie and 68 percent visited an amusement park. Another 51 percent watched a sport of some kind, 35 percent visited a museum and about 15 percent went to a jazz or classical music concert.

● Discuss the questions below with your classmates.

1. What did you do on the weekend?
- ▷ Did you go to the movies?
- ▷ Did you travel anywhere?
- ▷ Tell everyone about your weekend.

2. What is your favorite weekend activity?
- ▷ Why?

3. What kind of weekend do you like to have?
A busy and exciting one or a relaxing and quiet one?

4. What type of things do you have to do on the weekend?
- ▷ Go shopping?
- ▷ Go to the doctor or dentist?
- ▷ Take care of your brothers and sisters?
- ▷ Clean your house?

5. Do you have enough free time on the weekend?
- **No!**   Why not?

6. What are you going to do this Saturday?
- ▷ Tell everyone about your plan.

7. Where do young people in your country usually spend their weekend?

8. Do you want to see an action film this weekend?
- **No!**   Why not? What kind of movies do you want to see?

9. Do men and women spend their weekend differently?
- ▷ How?

10. If it were suddenly announced that tomorrow was a national holiday, what would you do?
- ▷ Tell everyone your opinion.

Super Speaking!

A. Listen to the conversation and practice with a partner. Use the cues given. Then change roles and practice again. Track 18

① on Saturday afternoon /
play tennis

 Did you do anything interesting on the weekend?

 Yeah! **On Saturday afternoon I played tennis.**

② on Sunday morning /
visit my grandparents

③ on Saturday night /
practice the drum

④ on Sunday morning /
go for a bicycle ride

B. Complete the chart below with your partner's information. Then tell the class about your partner's weekend.

Did you go to the movies last weekend?

No, I didn't.

So, what did you do?

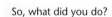

I went to the mountains with my dad.

Did you ...?	Yes	No	So, what did you do?
go shopping			
clean your room			
play soccer/baseball/tennis/badminton			
stay home and watch TV			
go to the countryside			
go out with friends			
go to an amusement park			

William didn't go to the movies. He went ...

Learn & Practice

- To form the **simple past of regular verbs**, we add *-ed* or *-d* to the base form of the verb.

- To make the **negative of the simple past**, we add *did not(= didn't)* before base verbs.

The US Civil War **started** in 1861 and **ended** in 1865.

Ann **didn't** play tennis this morning. She **helped** her mother clean the house.

- To make a **yes/no question**, we put *Did* at the beginning of the sentence. We always use the **base verb** after the subject.

Question
Did Jessica **listen** to K-pop music yesterday?

Yes, she did.

No, she didn't. She cleaned her room.

- Some verbs do not have *-ed* forms. They each have different changes. Their past forms are **irregular**.

Base form		Past form		Base form		Past form		Base form		Past form
buy	⇨	bought		sleep	⇨	slept		hear	⇨	heard
see	⇨	saw		teach	⇨	taught		sit	⇨	sat
go	⇨	went		ride	⇨	rode		meet	⇨	met
make	⇨	made		leave	⇨	left		speak	⇨	spoke
give	⇨	gave		fly	⇨	flew		take	⇨	took
have	⇨	had		find	⇨	found		drink	⇨	drank
come	⇨	came		wear	⇨	wore		stand	⇨	stood
eat	⇨	ate		lose	⇨	lost		write	⇨	wrote

Kevin **rode** his bicycle.

We **made** a model plane.

She **studied** for the chemistry test.

Super Speaking in Grammar Track 19

A. Listen to the conversation and practice with a partner. Use the cues given. Then change roles and practice again.

Ava / watch a DVD / ?
No ⇨ talk to Peter on the phone

 Did **Ava watched a DVD** last weekend?

No, she didn't. She **talked to Peter on the phone.**

Tiffany / go shopping / ?
No ⇨ read *the Lord of the Rings*

Steve / play baseball
No ⇨ paint a picture

They / visit Kyoto / ?
No ⇨ visit Seoul

B. Listen and repeat the dialog. Then use the speaking cards to practice it with your partner.

 Track 20

A: Did you have a nice weekend?

B: Not bad. I went ❶ ___to a new restaurant___ .

A: Oh yeah? What did you ❷ ___eat___ ?

B: I ate ❸ ___pasta and pizza___ .

❶ shopping with my sister
❷ buy
❸ a pair of pants and shoes

❶ to the movies
❷ see
❸ *Pirates of the Caribbean*

Describing People

**Read and listen to the conversation. Work in pairs.
Practice the conversation.** Track 21

Where is your sister Lisa?

That's her over there.

What does she look like?

She is tall. She has long blond hair and blue eyes. She is wearing a blue skirt.

✦ What does your favorite actor look like?　　✦ What does your mother or father look like?

A. Look at the pictures below. Then practice the conversation with your partner.

A: What does **Nancy** look like?
B: She has **short hair and blue eyes**.
　　She is wearing **a hat**.

| Nancy | Peter | Bob | Jessica |

short hair, blue eyes

a hat

straight hair, black eyes

a striped T-shirt

curl hair, brown eyes

jeans

long brown hair, blue eyes

a V-neck sweater

23

Reading Track 22

Sally or Paula?

NAME: Sally

She's five years old. She's intelligent, and she's got brown hair and brown eyes. She's got a small nose and a big smile. She's got four fingers and a thumb on her hand. She lives with her family. She hasn't got a big family, but she's got two sisters. She likes people and she loves her sisters and her friends. She loves chocolate and she likes bananas, too! Paula and Sally are similar, but Paula's a little girl, and Sally's a chimpanzee!

How are Sally and Paula different? Chimpanzees live in forests and people live in towns and cities. People drive cars, write books, play music, and use smartphones. But of course chimpanzees don't do these things. They use many different ways to communicate, such as facial expressions, body language, and kisses. They use stones to break hard nuts. They also use sticks to reach food, dig holes,

NAME: Paula

or attack enemies. So why are chimpanzees and people similar? Chimpanzees are closely related to humans. They share 98% of human DNA. It means that humans and chimpanzees shared a common ancestor. Sally and Paula look very different, but if we study the DNA, we see that they aren't very different at all.

finger	similar	forest	dig

A. Listen to these descriptions of people. Then check (✓) the correct picture. Track 23

1. a.  ☐

   b.  ☐

2. a.  ☐

   b. ☐

B. What do the students look like? Listen and make notes. ⊙ Track 24

	is ...	has ...	wearing ...
Cindy	tall, heavy		
Kelly			

C. Ask and answer questions about Cindy/Kelly with a partner.

A: Is Cindy tall and heavy?

B: Yes, she is.

A: Does she have reddish-blond hair?

B: No, she doesn't. She has curly brown hair.

A: What is she wearing?

B: She's wearing a red skirt and a blue blouse.

Dialog Track 25

Two students:
- Listen to the dialog and fill in the blanks.
- Listen again and check your answers.
- Read it together (change roles).

Steve	Wow, this _____ has great facilities.
Jessica	Yes, it does. All the members really love it.
Steve	You're _____. You must exercise _____.
Jessica	Thanks, I exercise three times a week with my best friend, Sunny. Can you see that girl over there wearing a _____?
Steve	So many girls are _____ headbands. Does she have _____?
Jessica	No, she doesn't. She has _____.
Steve	How about her height? Is she tall?
Jessica	She's about _____ and a little thin.
Steve	Oh, I think I can see her. She looks about 20 years old. Is that right?
Jessica	Yes, she is. And she's always _____.
Steve	I guess so. _____, who's the man talking to her? He has a _____. He is fat and bald. And he looks very old.
Jessica	Oh, that's Fred. He's her boss.
Steve	Oh, I see.

Two Types of Twins  Track 26

There are two types of twins, identical and non-identical. Identical twins are always the same sex and look exactly the same. Non-identical twins are not always the same sex. They look alike but they do not look exactly the same.

Sarah and Olivia are identical twins. They're 16 years old, and they're from Calgary, Canada. Sarah and Olivia are very similar, but they are not identical, especially in personality. The similarities? They're almost identical in appearance. They're both very friendly. But Sarah is very creative and imaginative - and romantic! Olivia is practical, analytical, and a little impatient.

● Discuss the questions below with your classmates.

1. What does your favorite teacher look like?

2. Tell your classmates about the people in your family. Describe their personality and appearance.

3. Describe your best friend. What kind of person is he/she? What does he/she look like?

4. Describe one of your classmates to your partner, and have him/her guess who you are describing.

5. Can you describe your girlfriend?
  ▶ Is she average, pretty or beautiful?

6. Describe your favorite (fe)male movie star. American or Korean?
  ▶ Why do you like him/her? Tell everyone about it.

Super Speaking!

A. Listen to the conversation and practice with a partner. Use the cues given. Then change roles and practice again. ⊙ Track 28

❶

Tiffany / a long dress /
short hair / ?
No ⇨ long curly hair

I'm looking for **Tiffany**.

Oh, she's wearing **a long dress**.

Does she have **short hair**?

No, she has **long curly hair**.

❷

Janet / a pink T-shirt /
short black hair / ?
No ⇨ long brown hair

❸

Sarah / a yellow striped
shirt / long blond hair / ?
No ⇨ long straight black
hair

B. Listen and repeat the dialog. Then use the speaking cards to practice it with your partner.

⊙ Track 29

A: Who is ❶ ____he____ ?

B: What does ❶ ____he____ look like?

A: ❶ ____He____ has ❷ ___long hair___. ❶ ____He____ 's
talking to the girl wearing ❸ ___a pair of glasses___.

B: Oh, that's ❹ ____Kevin____. I'll introduce ❺ ____him____
to you.

❶ she
❷ curly black hair
❸ sneakers
❹ Lisa
❺ her

❶ he
❷ short hair
❸ a skirt
❹ Steve
❺ him

Learn & Practice

- The **questions word** goes at the beginning of the question, followed by the verb and the subject.
- We use *what* to ask questions about **things**. We use *where* to ask questions about **location**. We use *who* to ask questions about **people**. We use *why* to ask questions about **reasons**. We use *how* to ask questions about **people's health or happiness**. We use *when* for questions about **time**.

Q: **What** are they?
A: They are birds.

Q: **Where** were you?
A: I was in the library.

Q: **How** are they?
A: They are happy.

Q: **Why** were you late?
A: I got up late.

＊We use 'What is he(she)?' to ask a question about his/her job.
  What is she? - She is a doctor.

Wh-word	Be	Subject		Answers
What	was	she?		She was an actress.
Where	is	Joe?		He is at home.
Who	is	she?		She is my girlfriend.
When	were	you	there?	I was there three years ago.
How	was	she	last night?	She was very sick.
Why	is	Kathy	happy?	Because she is going to the beach.

A. Make questions with *be*.

1. Where / John?

   ⇨ _Where is John?_

2. Why / they / hungry?

   ⇨ _____

3. How / the food?

   ⇨ _____

4. When / the concert?

   ⇨ _____

5. Why / you / late yesterday?

   ⇨ _____

6. Where / the station?

   ⇨ _____

Super Speaking in Grammar

A. Listen to the conversation and practice with a partner. Use the cues given. Then change roles and practice again. ◉ Track 30

Who / she / ?
⇨ my mother.

Who is she?

She is **my mother**.

Where / my laptop / ?
⇨ on the desk

What / she / ?
⇨ a police officer

How / the girls / ?
⇨ angry

B. Answer these questions about yourself.

1. What is your name?
   ⇨ _____

2. What was your grandfather?
   ⇨ _____

3. When is Christmas?
   ⇨ _____

4. When is your birthday?
   ⇨ _____

5. When is your father's birthday?
   ⇨ _____

6. How are you today?
   ⇨ _____

7. What is your favorite subject?
   ⇨ _____

8. What is your favorite sports?
   ⇨ _____

Unit 4 — Hobbies

Getting Ready

**Read and listen to the conversation. Work in pairs.
Practice the conversation.** Track 31

What are your hobbies?

My hobbies are watching movies, going inline-skating and listening to music.

* What do you like to do in your spare time?
* Do you like to blog online?

* What are your hobbies?
* Do you like to take photos?

A. Look at the pictures below. Then match the hobbies to each picture.

1. painting	2. surfing the Internet	3. listening to music	4. snowboarding
5. playing tennis	6. reading	7. inline skating	8. buying new clothes

31

What Are Your Favorite Hobbies?

Peter

Well, I like some sports, but I'm better at other things. I'm not good at football or rugby. I also like cooking. I usually cook for my family at the weekends. They really like it. Last week I made pasta with a special sauce. The activity I do best is playing music. I've got a band with my friends. A cousin of mine studies in the Royal Conservatory of Music in Canada. I think she is the best musician in our family! My favorite hobby is playing the trumpet.

Sarah

I hate sports. My favorite pastime is singing. I want to be famous. My mom sends me to a music school and I have a great singing teacher. She says that I'm really good at singing. I want to be the best singer when I grow up. I should work really hard to succeed. My school is the biggest school in the country, and some of the most famous singers in the world studied there too! So, I think I've got a good chance.

John

I've got a younger sister. Her name is Jennifer. We are very friendly and never fight. We get along but we have got different tastes. I'm a very active boy. I love outdoor activities. I enjoy cycling, skateboarding, playing soccer and swimming. But what I really like is surfing. It's exciting and fun. My friends and I usually go surfing after school and at weekends. In the future I want to be a professional surfer, so I always practice two hours a day. My sister is very calm and quiet. She prefers indoor activities. She doesn't like surfing or playing soccer. She loves reading, dancing, listening to K-pop music and surfing the Internet. But there's one thing we both like doing. We like watching adventure movies and cartoons. I definitely love Harry Potter's movies.

A. Write the correct words under each picture. Use the words from the box.

dancing

singer

rugby

musician

cycling

skateboarding

1.

_____

2.

_____

3.

_____

4.

_____

5.

_____

6.

_____

Super Activity!

A. People are talking about hobbies and pastimes. Listen and number the correct pictures. Track 33

1.

☐

2.

☐

4.

☐

B. Listen and check (✓) the correct answer. Track 34

1. _____ a. I go there by bicycle.

   _____ b. I go snowboarding twice a week.

2. _____ a. My hobby is surfing the Internet and playing soccer.

   _____ b. Yes, It keeps me healthy.

3. _____ a. I enjoy listening to K-pop music.

   _____ b. Tennis is the most boring sport I've seen.

Dialog ⊙ Track 35

Two students:
- Listen to the dialog and fill in the blanks.
- Listen again and check your answers.
- Read it together (change roles).

Alice	William, what is your _____ cartoon?
William	My favorite animation cartoon is *Dooly*.
Alice	_____ ?
William	Because the character is very cute.
Alice	What do you like to do _____ ?
William	I like to _____. Have you ever tried inline skating?
Alice	Yes, I have. I have a pair of inline skates at home.
	I _____ inline skating, too.
William	Then, _____ us this Saturday?
	I'm going to go inline skating with my friends at a skating rink.
Alice	Sure, I'd love that. _____
	me to meet you?
William	Come to _____ in front of
	the skating rink _____.
Alice	Okay. I'll see you then.

Answer the Questions

Check (√) T for true or F for false.

	T	F
1. William's favorite animation cartoon is *Tom and Jerry*.	☐	☐
2. Alice is going to go hiking tomorrow morning.	☐	☐
3. Alice decided to go inline skating with William this Saturday.	☐	☐
4. They're going to meet at the library by 10:00.	☐	☐

● Discuss the questions below with your classmates.

1. What is your hobby?
  ▶ Why do you like it?
  ▶ Tell everyone about it.

2. How long have you had your hobby?
  ▶ How many hours a week do you spend on your hobby?

3. Do you like to go inline skating?
  `Yes!` ○ Why?
  `No!` ○ Why not?

4. How much money do your hobbies cost you?
  ▶ With whom do you enjoy your hobbies?

5. Have you ever tried snowboarding or skiing?
  `Yes!` Where? When? Tell everyone about it.
  `No!` Do you want to?

6. Does your father or mother have a hobby?
  ▶ Does anyone in your family have an interesting hobby?

7. Why do people have hobbies?
  ▶ Why do people need hobbies?
  ▶ Tell everyone your opinions.

8. Which hobbies are the most expensive?
  ▶ Which hobbies are the cheapest?
  ▶ Which hobbies cost nothing at all?

9. Do you make friends with people who have the same hobbies?

10. Did you ever recommend that family members share your hobbies with you?

Super Speaking!

A. Listen to the conversation and practice with a partner. Use the cues given. Then change roles and practice again. ⊙ Track 37

skateboarding / ?
school / gloves

How about going **skateboarding**?

I'd love to. Where do you want to meet?

In front of the **school**. And you must wear **gloves**.

bowling / ?
parking lot / jeans

fishing / ?
bakery / a hat

jogging / ?
park / sneakers

B. Practice the conversation with your partner, using the words or phrases in the table.

What hobbies did you use to have?

I used to listen to K-pop music.

What hobbies do you have now?

Well, I like playing the guitar.

Your turn to ask now!

play computer games	go inline skating
collect coins/stamps	keep pets
go fishing	go skiing/snowboarding
listen to music	go swimming
watch a movie on TV	surf the Internet

- Like a noun or a pronoun, we use an **infinitive** as an **object** of certain verbs and constructions.

He tried **to give** him his medicine, but he refused **to open** his mouth.

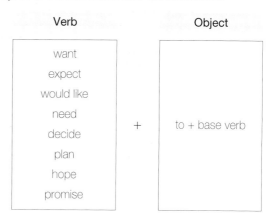

Verb		Object
want		
expect		
would like		
need	+	to + base verb
decide		
plan		
hope		
promise		

- We can use a **gerund** or an **infinitive** after certain verbs. The meaning is the **same**.

Jason loves **waterskiing** in the Atlantic.
= He loves to **waterski** in the Atlantic.

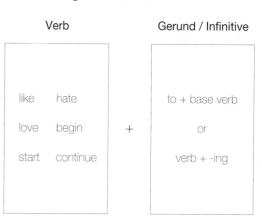

Verb			Gerund / Infinitive
like	hate		to + base verb
love	begin	+	or
start	continue		verb + -ing

A. Complete the sentences with the gerund or infinitive of the verb in brackets. Sometimes two answers are possible.

1. Are you planning _____ (take) a vacation this year?

2. I want _____ (meet) my grandparents.

3. He started _____ (drive) when he was 18 years old.

4. I hope _____ (watch) TV in English.

5. Peter decided _____ (study) Korean.

6. Karen doesn't like _____ (sing) in front of other people.

Super Speaking in Grammar

A. Listen to the conversation and practice with a partner. Use the cues given. Then change roles and practice again. ⊙ Track 38

❶

listen to music
⇨ learn about different cultures

In my free time, I enjoy **listening to music**. How about you?

I like **learning about different cultures**.

❷

play volleyball
⇨ draw cartoons

❸

ride my bicycle
⇨ travel around the country

❹

spend time with my friends
⇨ jog in the park

B. Work with a partner. Tell your partner about three places you want to go to and what you expect to see there.

I want to go to Paris. I expect to see the Eiffel Tower.

Your turn to now!

Paris / the Eiffel Tower

London / the clock tower

Seoul / the Seoul Tower

Italy / the Leaning Tower of Pisa

Rome / the Colosseum

New York / the Statue of Liberty

Getting Ready

Read and listen to the conversation. Work in pairs. Practice the conversation. Track 39

What's your favorite movie?

I like comedies the best. I really don't like horror movies.

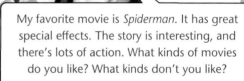

My favorite movie is *Spiderman*. It has great special effects. The story is interesting, and there's lots of action. What kinds of movies do you like? What kinds don't you like?

⚜ What kinds of movies do you like?　　⚜ When did you last see a movie?

⚜ What do you think of Korean/Hollywood movies?

A. Look at the pictures below. Then write the correct kind of movies under each picture.

 1.	 2.	 3.	 4.	 5.	 6.
_____	_____	_____	_____	_____	_____

horror	animated movie	action movie	comedy	romance	science fiction

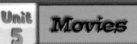

A Famous Writer

J.K. Rowling is a very famous writer. If you don't know her, you probably heard about her fiction book called *Harry Potter* that in 2001 became a movie ending up in 2011. Millions of children, teenagers, men and women read her books. Her books have been translated into 65 languages and have sold over 350 million copies.

Before the *Harry Potter* Series, she was very poor. She went to a coffee shop to write the stories. She said, "Suddenly, Harry's character and an evil sorcerer, Voldemort just came into my mind." After a few years writing, she finally finished her first book in 1996. She sent it to many publishers, but most publishers didn't like it. Finally, someone wanted to sell her book. In 1997, *Harry Potter and the Sorcerer's Stone* was in the bookstores. The publisher said, "This is a book for children. Adults won't read it. You won't make a lot of money." The publisher was wrong. Her book became a best-selling book around the world. *Harry Potter* books became very popular for both children and adults. Where is she from? Where does she live? How does she write her books?

J.K. Rowling is from Britain, and she lives with her husband, son and daughter in Scotland. Writing is her hobby and her work. She always writes with a pen first, and then with her computer. She sometimes watches TV: she really likes cartoons. Harry Potter is always the hero in her books. Of course she likes him a lot! Today she became an international person and one of the richest women in the U.K. but at the same time she is so thankful that she donates most of her fortune to charity foundations.

Harry Potter is ten years old and he's very unhappy. His mother and father are dead and he lives with his aunt and uncle. Harry doesn't like them or their son Dudley at all. One day, Harry gets a letter from Hogwarts, a school for wizards! At Hogwarts, Harry is very famous and popular. He learns magic and plays a game called 'Quidditch'. Harry's very happy there.

A. Match these words with the pictures.

1.

2.

3.

4.

5.

6.

teenagers	_____
character	_____
sorcerer	_____
sell	_____
writer	_____
translate	_____

Super Activity!

A. Listen to the dialogs and write the number in the correct poster. Track 41

1.

2.

3.

B. Listen agin check your answers. Track 42

C. Listen to the conversation. Then circle the picture that does not belong. Track 43

a.

b.

c.

d.

Dialog Track 44

Two students:

- Listen to the dialog and fill in the blanks.
- Listen again and check your answers.
- Read it together (change roles).

Woman	Excuse me, I'm _____ for Film Magic Magazine. Can I ask you a few questions?
Edward	Sure.
Carol	_____?
Woman	Thanks. _____ your friends?
Edward	Yes, we do. We go _____.
Woman	What kind of movies do you watch?
Carol	I watch all kinds of movies but _____ are my favorite! They're so _____!
Edward	No, they aren't.
Carol	Edward doesn't like science-fiction movies very much.
Edward	I don't like science fiction movies at all. I like _____.
Woman	Do you like _____?
Edward	Of curse! I think they're very funny.
Woman	What about you?
Carol	No way! They're for kids. They're _____.
Woman	Okay. Thanks a lot. _____ for the movie theater tonight.
Edward	Great! Is it a horror movie?
Woman	No, it's an animated film.
Carol	Oh no!
Edward	Don't worry, Carol. I can go with Jane ... he, he, he.

funny

boring

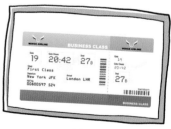

ticket

Super Discussion!

● Track 45

● Discuss the questions below with your classmates.

1. What is your favorite Korean movie?
- ▶ What is it about?
- ▶ Tell everyone your opinions.
- ▶ What kind of movies do your parents like?

2. What do you think of Korean movies?

3. Are there any kinds of movies you dislike?
- ▶ If so, what kinds?   ▶ Why do you dislike them?

4. What is the best movie you have ever seen?
- ▶ Who was in it?   ▶ Why did you like it?
- ▶ Who was the director?
- ▶ What is the worst movie you have ever seen?

5. Do you think movie stars make too much money?
- Yes! Why?   No! Why not?
- ▶ Support your opinion.

6. Would you like to be a movie star or a film director?
- Yes! Why?   No! Why not?
- ▶ Who are your favorite male/female Korean movie stars?

7. Do you like a horror movie? What is the scariest movies you have ever seen?
- ▶ What's the funniest?   ▶ What's the most romantic?

8. How often do you go to a movie theater?
- ▶ Do you usually watch movies at the theater or watch them at home?

Talk It Over

● What do you think of these ideas? Check(√) your thoughts. Then talk with your classmates.

	Yes	No
1. Hollywood movies are responsible for the behavior of today's youth.		
2. There is too much violence in movies.		
3. Movie stars make so much more money than teachers and firefighters.		

Super Speaking!

A. Listen to the conversation and practice with a partner. Use the cues given. Then change roles and practice again. ⦿ Track 46

cultures and languages
⇨ horror movies

 I like movies from different countries.

 What do you like about them?

 Well, I can learn about different **cultures and languages**. What kind of movies do you usually see?

 I like **horror movies**.

customs and traditions
⇨ romantic movies

cultures and life styles
⇨ action movies

things that I never knew before
⇨ science fiction movies

B. Listen and repeat the dialog. Then use the speaking cards to practice it with your partner.

⦿ Track 47

A: Do you like to go to the movies?

B: Yes, I like movies a lot.

A: What kind of movies do you like best?

B: I like ❶ ___adventure movies___. How about you?

A: I like ❷ ___comedies___ very much.

B: Who is your favorite movie star?

A: I like ❸ ___John Candy___. How about you?

B: I'm a big fan of ❹ ___Harrison Ford___.

❶ scary movies
❷ comedies
❸ Arnold Schwarzenegger
❹ Megan Fox

❶ thrillers
❷ animated movies
❸ Brad Pitt
❹ Julia Roberts

Learn & Practice

- We use the form of *have(has)*+past participle for the present perfect.

- We use the **present perfect** for an action or situation that **happened at some unspecified time in the past**. The exact time is not mentioned because it is not important. We put more emphasis on the action.

Joseph and Ava **have bought** a new sports car.
(When did they buy it? We don't mention the exact time because it isn't important. What is important is the fact that they've got a new sports car.)

- We can use the **present perfect** to talk about an action or situation that **started in the past and continues up to the present**. We use *for* and *since* with the present perfect to talk about **how long the action or situation existed from the past to the present**. We use *for* to talk about **a length of time**; we use *since* to talk about **when a period of time began**.

Kimberly has been an English teacher **since** 2011.
She has studied English **for** 15 years.
(She started working as an English teacher in 2011 and she still is a teacher.)

A. Complete the sentences with the present perfect of the verbs in brackets.

1. Nancy ___has work___ (work) in France.

2. They _____ (be) to Mexico City.

3. He _____ (finish) breakfast.

4. It _____ (rain) for three days.

5. We _____ (eat) lunch.

6. My dad _____ (give up) smoking.

B. Complete the sentences with *for* or *since*.

1. Diana and Jordan have been married _____ twenty-two years.

2. Betty has been a teacher _____ 1999.

3. Julie is at the school gym. She has been there _____ 10:00 this morning.

4. Jason has taught English _____ twenty years.

Super Speaking in Grammar

A. Listen to the conversation and practice with a partner. Use the cues given. Then change roles and practice again. ◉ Track 48

Cynthia / buy a new camera / ?
No ➪ a new smartphone

 Has **Cynthia bought a new camera?**

 No, she hasn't. She has bought **a new smartphone.**

Jessica / travel by bicycle / ?
No ➪ by train

they / live in England / ?
No ➪ in Korea

Lauren / lose her phone / ?
No ➪ her passport

B. Work with a partner. Ask and answer questions, using the phrases given.

Have you eaten Italian food?

No, I haven't eaten Italian food.

Yes, I've eaten Italian food.

Your turn to ask now!

eat Italian food	try windsurfing
ride a horse	finish your homework
see the Statue of Liberty	write an e-mail to your teacher
take yoga lessons	live in this city for 10 years

Weather

Read and listen to the conversation. Work in pairs. Practice the conversation. Track 49

What does the paper say the weather's going to be like?

It will be fair but occasionally cloudy.

What is your favorite season?

My favorite season is summer. Because I can see nice sunshine.

How is the weather today?

What is your favorite season?

What is your favorite weather?

Do you believe the weather forecast on TV?

A. Look at the weather pictures. Then write the weather words with the pictures.

1.
_____

2.
_____

3.
_____

4.
_____

5.
_____

wind and rainy   cool and sunny   cold and snowy   warm and cloudy   hot and humid

47

Seasons

Spring, summer, autumn, and winter are the four seasons of the year. Which is my favorite one? Of course summer! Why? Let me tell you. I like the other seasons as well, but summer is the best for me. I think all children love summer because of long school holidays and I'm no exception. I don't have to wake up early and go to school.

Summer comes after spring and it is the hottest season of the year. The sun shines brightly, the sky is rarely cloudy, and the water in the sea becomes warm enough to swim. Even if it becomes too hot, you can always go for a walk in the shady woods. I also like summer because there are many berries, fruit and vegetables, not to mention numerous flowers in the fields.

Sometimes the air in summer becomes stuffy, but occasional thunderstorms bring relief. After the thunderstorms, the air becomes remarkably fresh and very often we can see the rainbow in the sky. The sky is always blue and it hardly ever rains, and if it does, it is a warm and pleasant rain. I usually enjoy walking in the rain because it relaxes me. The days are long and very hot. The sun is strong in summer, but it's nice early in the morning and late in the afternoon. People wear light clothes and spend most of their time outdoors. I also enjoy my free time, playing with my friends, watching TV, and doing other fun activities. In summer, everybody takes a holiday. People go to different places for their holiday, but many people go to the beach. They can enjoy swimming and playing beach ball. Everybody has a nice time in summer and a good rest, too.

A. Write the correct words under each picture. Use the words from the box.

children

winter

holiday

spring

wake up

field

1.

_____

2.

_____

3.

_____

4.

_____

5.

_____

6.

_____

Super Activity!

A. Listen and write the numbers under the correct pictures. 🔘 Track 51

1.

☐

2.

☐

3.

☐

4.

☐

B. Will they stay inside or go outside? Listen and check the correct answers. 🔘 Track 52

	Jennifer	Gregory	Louis	Steven
Stay inside	_____	_____	_____	_____
Go outside	_____	_____	_____	_____

Dialog ● Track 53

Two students:
- Listen to the dialog and fill in the blanks.
- Listen again and check your answers.
- Read it together (change roles).

Wilson	Hi, Nancy. It's me.
Nancy	Hi, Wilson. _____?
Wilson	Great. I'm having a great time. The _____. Every day is warm, sunny, and great. I sleep late and go to the beach. How's it there?
Nancy	_____ the hurricane in Seoul _____?
Wilson	No, What was it like?
Nancy	Well, the hurricane _____. There was a lot of rain and strong winds. Many _____.
Wilson	Hurricane? I _____. You should be here with me. Is the weather still bad now?
Nancy	No. The storm has finished, and the wind and rain _____. It's _____ here today.

The Differences Between ℃ and ℉ ● Track 54

Temperature can be measured in degrees Centigrade or degrees Fahrenheit. Usually we use ℃ to stand for Centigrade or Celsius. The abbreviation for Fahrenheit is ℉. The sign for degrees is "°". Centigrade or Celsius is commonly used in Korea, while Fahrenheit is widely used in English speaking countries.

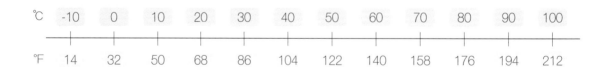

℃	-10	0	10	20	30	40	50	60	70	80	90	100
℉	14	32	50	68	86	104	122	140	158	176	194	212

1. The freezing point of water is 0℃ or 32 ℉.
2. The boilig point of water is 100℃ or 212 ℉.
3. The normal body temperature is 37℃ or 98.6 ℉.
4. The temperature on a warm spring day is 15℃ or 59 ℉.
5. The temperature on a hot summer's day is 35℃ or 95 ℉.

Super Discussion!  Track 55

- Discuss the questions below with your classmates.

1. Do you like sunny weather?

Yes! → Why? Tell everyone your opinion.

No! → Why not? What is your favourite weather?

2. What do you think of today's weather?

▷ Do you like rainy weather?

▷ What is your favorite season? Why do you like it?

3. Do you moods change with weather?

Yes! Why? No! Why not?

4. What is a weather forecast?

▷ Do you believe the news reports?

▷ Do you always try and look at or read the weather forecast?

5. What was your favorite time of year when you were younger?

▷ Why did you like it?

6. You wake up, look outside, and see a warm, sunny day in the spring.

In other words, it's perfect. What will you likely do?

▷ Please explain.

7. Do you worry about the world's changing weather?

Yes! Tell everyone your opinion.

No! Tell everyone your opinion.

8. Have you ever experienced extreme weather?

Yes! What happened? Tell everyone your experience.

Have you been in any really bad weather?

Talk It Over

- What do you think of these ideas? Check(✓) your thoughts. Then talk with your classmates.

	Yes	No
1. Many icebergs are melting because of global warming.		
2. Many disasters in our country are caused by weather.		
3. In recent years, we are losing our four distinct seasons.		

51

Super Speaking!

A. Listen to the conversation and practice with a partner. Use the cues given. Then change roles and practice again. (●) Track 56

Alaska / cold, snowy
⇨ take a coat

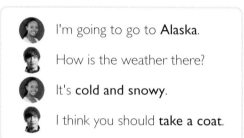

I'm going to go to **Alaska**.

How is the weather there?

It's **cold and snowy**.

I think you should **take a coat**.

Cairo / hot, dry
⇨ pack sunglasses

Bali / sunny, hot
⇨ take a sunscreen

London / windy, cold
⇨ take a muffler and gloves

B. Ask your classmates about their favorite season and why they like it. Complete the chart.

What is your favorite season?

My favorite season is summer.

Why do you like the season?

Because I can go to the beach with my family.

Name	Spring	Summer	Fall	Winter	Reason

Learn & Practice

- When we compare **three or more people or things**, we use the **superlative form** of adjectives and adverbs. We use the definite article *the* before superlative adjectives and adverbs.
- After **superlatives**, we often use *in* before **the names of places** such as the world, countries and cities; and with **group nouns** such as the class, my family and the group.
- After **superlatives**, we often use *of* before **expressions of time and quantity, and plural nouns**.

Superlative:
adjective/adverb + -est

A cheetah is **the fastest** animal in the world.

Superlative:
most + adjective/adverb

Ava is **the most** intelligent of the three sisters.

● Spelling rules of the superlative forms

	Adjective		Comparative		Superlative	
One-syllable adjectives + -est	tall	large	taller	larger	tallest	largest
	cheap	long	cheaper	longer	cheapest	longest
double consonant + -est	big	hot	bigger	hotter	biggest	hottest
	thin		thinner		thinnest	
drop y + -iest	easy	heavy	easier	heavier	easiest	heaviest
	pretty	happy	prettier	happier	prettiest	happiest
For most 2 or more syllable adjectives, **most** is used.	difficult		more difficult		most difficult	
	famous		more famous		most famous	
	popular		more popular		most popular	
	interesting		more interesting		most interesting	

	Adverb	Comparative	Superlative
Most is used with adverbs that end in -ly.	carefully	**more** carefully	**most** carefully
	beautifully	**more** beautifully	**most** beautifully
Adverb + -est	hard	harder	hardest
	fast	faster	fastest

	Adjective (adverb)	Comparative	Superlative
Irregular	good (well)	better	best
	bad, ill (badly)	worse	worst
	many, much	more	most
	little	less	least

Super Speaking in Grammar

A. Listen to the conversation and practice with a partner. Use the cues given. Then change roles and practice again. ⊙ Track 57

① big desert / in the world / ?
⇨ the Sahara

> What is **the biggest desert in the world?**
>
> I think **the Sahara** is the biggest desert in the world.

② big / of all birds / ?
⇨ the ostrich

③ poisonous snake / in the world / ?
⇨ the rattle-snake

④ far planet / from the sun / ?
⇨ Pluto

B. Work with a partner. Look at the information below and make superlatives, as in the example.

> Alaska is the largest state in the USA.

> Your turn now.

Alaska	high	state	country		
the sun				the USA	South Korea
Mt. Halla	large	planet	mountain		
China				Brazil	our solar system
Yao Ming	long	basketball	player		
the Amazon River	tall	river		China	Asia

Summer Plans

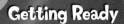**Getting Ready**

Read and listen to the conversation. Work in pairs. Practice the conversation. (●) Track 58

> What are you doing this summer?

> I'm taking a vacation with my family.

> Where are you going?

> My dad promised to go to Haeundae! I'm so excited.

⟿ What are you doing this summer?
⟿ What are you doing next Saturday?

⟿ What are you planning for the weekend?
⟿ What are you doing after school today?

A. Look at the pictures below. Then match the correct phrases to each picture.

 □

 □

 □

 □

 □

 □

 □

 □

1. traveling to Dokdo
2. going to the beach
3. visiting the Stature of Liberty
4. going fishing
5. going camping with my family
6. traveling with my girlfriend
7. spending time with my friends
8. staying at home

Summer Vacation Plan

Hi, I am Richard. My summer vacation is coming soon. I am so happy to make a summer plan. First, I will do my homework carefully. Second, I am going to help my mother with housework. Then, I want to play with my best friend. I will also have a trip with my parents. I think every day will be happy during my summer vacation. I am sure I will have a wonderful vacation. I can't wait.

Hi, I am Cindy. I am a singer. I'm taking a long vacation this summer! I thought about going to Greece or Spain, but decided on Korea. I always take vacations in Asia. This time I want to do something different. I heard that Korea is beautiful, and I know there are many people there who speak English. I'm going to Gyeongpo Lake in Gangwon-do. I'm leaving the first week in June and staying until September. I plan to have a very relaxing vacation. I'm taking walks, going fishing, and going bike riding. I'm planning to spend time in the beautiful countryside. I love nature. I hope I can forget all my problems! A great vacation! I can't wait.

Summer Camp  Track 60

In many countries summer camps for children are very popular. In Canada and the USA some of the summer camps are in the countryside or on lakes. The children stay there for one or four weeks and sleep in tents or cabins. In the morning they get up for good breakfast. Then they do arts and crafts activities, sports activities or music. Sometimes they go for long walks in the forest or trips in canoes. Often in the evening, they gather around a big campfire to sing songs or tell stories.

Building Vocabulary

A. Write the correct words under each picture. Use the words from the box.

leave
cabin
housework
trip
plan
take walks

1.

_____

2.

_____

3.

_____

4.

_____

5.

_____

6.

_____

Super Activity!

A. Listen to the conversations and number the pictures. Track 61

1.

☐

2.

☐

3.

☐

B. Listen and draw each line to the correct picture. Track 62

Patrick	Wendy	Scott

a.

b.

c.

Dialog Track 63

Two students:
- Listen to the dialog and fill in the blanks.
- Listen again and check your answers.
- Read it together (change roles).

Gloria	Do you have _____ for this summer?
Joseph	Yes. I'm going to go camping with my family.
Gloria	I've never gone to camp. _____?
Joseph	We will do many exciting things. In the morning, we go _____. In the afternoon, we play _____. We sit around a campfire at night. We sing or _____.
Gloria	That sounds wonderful.
Joseph	It is wonderful. _____?
Gloria	I'm visiting Thailand. My aunt _____ there.
Joseph	Sounds great! _____?
Gloria	On August 8. I'm staying there _____.
Joseph	Good for you! There are many wonderful places in Thailand, right?
Gloria	Yes, there are. Thailand is _____.

Pair Work Ask and answer the questions about the dialog with your partner.

1. What's Joseph doing for this summer?
   ⇨ He's going to _____.

2. What exciting things is Joseph going to do there?
   ⇨ In the morning, he's going to _____ and _____. In the afternoon, he's going to _____ or _____. At night, he's going to _____ and tell _____.

3. Why is Gloria visiting Thailand?
   ⇨ Her aunt _____.

● Discuss the questions below with your classmates.

1. In the summer, which place do you prefer - the mountains or the sea?
   ▸ Explain to everyone.
   ▸ Do you prefer summer or winter vacations? Why?

2. Do you have any special plans for this summer?
   ▸ Tell everyone about them.

3. Do you like to take vacations with family or friends?
   Yes!   Why?
   No!   Why not?

4. Are there any special events that take place in summer in your country?
   ▸ Talk about them together.

5. Where did you spend your last summer vacation?
   ▸ What did you do? Would you always go to the same place or different places?
   ▸ Tell everyone about it.

6. What are you going to do this weekend?

7. If you were going on a camping trip for a week, what ten things would you bring?
   ▸ Explain why.

8. Do schools, temples, or churches have special programs for this summer?

Talk It Over

● What do you think of these ideas? Check(✓) your thoughts. Then talk with your classmates.

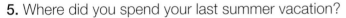

	Yes	No
1. The summer job is a tradition among students of Korean universities.		
2. Vacations can help you stay healthier by reducing stress.		
3. Do you think summer camps are important for kids?		

Super Speaking!

A. Listen to the conversation and practice with a partner. Use the cues given. Then change roles and practice again. Track 65

❶

this weekend / ?
⇨ babysit my baby

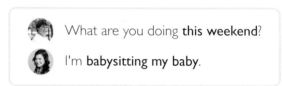

What are you doing **this weekend**?

I'm **babysitting my baby**.

②

next week / ?
⇨ leave my old apartment and
I'm throwing a moving party

③

tonight / ?
⇨ call my family for a
barbecue banquet

④

next Sunday / ?
⇨ go to the beach / Would
you like to come?

B. Listen and repeat the dialog. Then use the speaking cards to practice it with your partner.

 Track 66

A: What are you doing this summer?

B: I'm ❶ ___traveling to Dok-do___.

A: Sounds wonderful! Who are you going to travel with?

B: With ❷ ___my family___. How about you?

A: I'm ❸ ___visiting Namsan hanok village___.

B: Enjoy your time there.

A: Thank you.

❶ visit the Stature
of Liberty

❷ my friends

❸ visit my uncle in
Thailand

❶ go to Hawaii for
two weeks

❷ my sisters

❸ visit my brother in
Poland.

Learn & **Practice**

- We can use the **present progressive** to talk about future actions and events that are **already planned** or **decided**.

- We often use verbs like *go, come, see, meet, stay, have, leave*. The **present progressive** for the future and *be going to* have similar meanings.

Ava **is flying** to Singapore in two hours. She is at the airport now.

My friends **are getting** married next week. I'm really excited.

- We can often use **present participles** and **past participles** of verbs as **adjectives**. They can play role of an adjective. Like other adjective, they modify nouns or describe the subjects.

Present Participle: **verb + -ing**
- It is used to describe the person or thing that produces the feeling.

Past Participle: **verb + -ed**
- It is used to describe someone's feelings.

The soccer game was **exciting**.

They were **excited** during the game.

The loud noise was **frightening**.

He was **frightened** by the loud noise.

A. Rewrite the sentences using the present progressive.

1. We are going to leave for our trip at 10:00 tomorrow.

⇨ *We are leaving for our trip at 10:00 tomorrow.*

2. My father and I are going to fly to Tokyo.

⇨ _____

3. My sister is going to meet us there.

⇨ _____

Super Speaking in Grammar

A. Listen to the conversation and practice with a partner. Use the cues given. Then change roles and practice again. ⦿ Track 67

tonight / ?
⇨ go to an ice hockey match

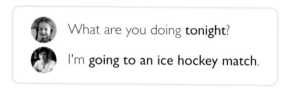

What are you doing **tonight**?

I'm **going to an ice hockey match**.

tomorrow / ?
⇨ meet an important buyer from
England tomorrow

after school today / ?
⇨ learn Latin dance at the
Latin Culture Center

for the vacation / ?
⇨ learn Turkish at the Istanbul
Culture Center

B. Work with a partner. Ask your partner questions using the present progressive. Share some of your answers with the class.

What are you doing tonight?

I'm staying home and watching a movie on TV.

Your turn to ask!

what / do / tonight	where / go / after school	what time / have dinner
what time / get up / tomorrow	when / go / to bed tonight	what / do / tomorrow
what / do / this weekend	what / do / after school today	what / do / on Saturday evening

Transportation

Read and listen to the conversation. Work in pairs. Practice the conversation. Track 68

How do you get to school, Peter?

I ride my bicycle to school every day.

How long does it take?

It only takes about ten minutes.

How do you get to school/work?

How often do you use public transportation?

How long does it take you to get there?

What do you think is the safest kind of transportation? Why?

A. Look at the pictures below. Then match the correct phrases to each picture. Listen and check your answers. Track 69

1. drive my car ___e___

2. take a taxi _____

3. take the subway _____

4. catch the bus _____

5. ride my bicycle _____

6. walk _____

a.

b.

c.

d.

e.

f.

How Do Students Around the World Get to School?

In North America, most students go to school by bus. The subway is also widely used in some cities. In small towns and cities, some students walk or ride bicycles to school. The yellow school bus is a familiar vehicle all over North America. It is a very convenient form of transportation because it takes students right to the entrance to the school. It also gives students opportunity to chat with their friends. However, the bus is slow and does not always pick up on time. The subway is a means of getting around quickly in many cities. However, it is expensive and can be very crowded during rush hour. Another disadvantage of

the subway is that the stops are not so close to the school, so students often have to walk considerable distances or take a bus from the subway stop to the school. Walking has a number of advantages for those who live

reasonably close to school. It's free and it provides a form of exercise. However, it's no fun if you have a large backpack full of books to carry. It's also unpleasant if the weather is either too hot or cold or wet. In other parts of the world, things are different. In Japan, most students take trains to school, although others also walk or ride their bicycles. In China, it depends on where you are. In big cities, students usually ride their bicycles to school or take buses. For many students, it is easy to get to school, but in places where there are rivers and lakes, students usually go to school by boat. That must be a lot more fun than taking a bus.

A. Write the correct words under each picture. Use the words from the box.

convenience

backpack

subway

transportation

entrance

crowded

1.

_____

2.

_____

3.

_____

4.

_____

5.

_____

6.

_____

Super Activity!

A. Listen and check (✓) the most suitable answers. Track 71

1. a. _____ I don't have to go to school.
   b. _____ No, I ride my bicycle to the subway station. Then I take the subway.

2. a. _____ You should take the train at 6 p.m.
   b. _____ There are no tickets available today.

3. a. _____ I took an express bus.
   b. _____ It's too far to walk there.

B. Listen and write the distance. Then check your answers with your partner. Track 72

1.

_____

2.

_____

3.

_____

Transportation

Dialog Track 73

Two students:

● Listen to the dialog and fill in the blanks.
● Listen again and check your answers.
● Read it together (change roles).

Man Let me see now. Which train _____ to get on?

Woman Excuse me. Do you need any help?

Man Yes, I want to go to Seoul Tower, but I'm really lost. _____ to Korea, so I have no idea on _____ the trains.

Woman First, you need to buy a ticket _____. Then take subway line 4.

Man Line number 4, alright. Oh, and _____ this time of day?

Woman Usually, they come about _____ or so.

Man Alright. And where do I get off the train?

Woman Get off at Myeong-dong Station, five stops from here. The sign at the station is _____, so you'll be able to read it. Access by taxi or car is prohibited, so you'll have to walk, take a bus, or cable car. From Myeong-dong Station, _____ to the cable car platform. The way up by cable car offers a great view of Seoul and a pleasant ride. You _____ bus at Chungmu-ro Station (Line 3 or 4) or at Dongguk University Station (Line 3), which will take you to the parking lot of Seoul Tower. The bus runs regularly, so you can take it from wherever it is most convenient. Even the bus ride up the winding road affords a nice view of the mountain. The number 2 bus will _____ right below Seoul Tower. After completing your tour, take the same bus at the bus stop _____. There is a bus every 6 minutes from 8 a.m. to 12 a.m.

Man I got it. Thanks for your help.

Woman No problem. Good luck0

Super Discussion!  Track 74

● Discuss the questions below with your classmates.

1. What do you usually ride when you go to school or work?
- ▶ What else can you ride to get to your school or work?
- ▶ How much is the bus fare or the train fare?

2. How long does it take for you to get to school or your office?
- ▶ Which is the best way to get to school in your own opinion?

3. Do you have a bicycle? If so, how often do you use it? If not, do you want one?
- ▶ If so, when did you get it?
- ▶ How often do you ride it?
- ▶ How much did it cost?
- ▶ What color is it?

4. Do you often ride public transportation during rush hour?
- `Yes!` How often?
- `No!` Why not? Tell everyone your reason.
- ▶ How do you feel about spending time in your car during rush hour?

5. Do you prefer to travel by land, by sea, or by air? Why?
- ▶ Please explain.
- ▶ What can you suggest to make traveling in Korea more comfortable?

6. Do you always wear a seat belt?
- ▶ Even if you are riding in the rear seat?
- ▶ How about on a bus?

7. What do you usually do when riding a train or bus?
- ▶ Do you read?
- ▶ Do you sleep?

8. Is the public transportation in your country good?
- `Yes!` Why?
- `No!` Why not?

Talk It Over

● What do you think of these ideas? Check(√) your thoughts. Then talk with your classmates.

	Yes	No
1. Do you think that speed cameras help to reduce traffic accidents?		
2. Should people stop using fossil fuels for transit and start using renewable energy sources?		

Super Speaking!

A. Listen to the conversation and practice with a partner. Use the cues given. Then change roles and practice again. Track 75

❶

walk
⇨ 30 minutes to walk

 How do you get to school?

 I usually **walk**.

 How long does it take from home to school?

 It takes about **30 minutes to walk**.

take the subway
⇨ 10 minutes by subway

catch a taxi
⇨ 20 minutes by taxi

ride my bicycle
⇨ 5 minutes / I live close to the school

B. Complete the chart with the information about how you and two of your classmates get to school. Who has the longest trip? Who has the shortest? Share your information with your classmates.

How do you get to school?

How long does it take you?

How far is it?

I take the school bus.

It takes thirty minutes.

It's about 10 kilometers.

Name	How?	How long?	How far?
1.			
2.			
3.			
4.			

Learn & Practice

- We use the **passive** when we are more interested in **what happened than who did it**. The actor (subject) of the verb comes after *by*. The object of the active voice sentence becomes the subject of the passive voice sentence.

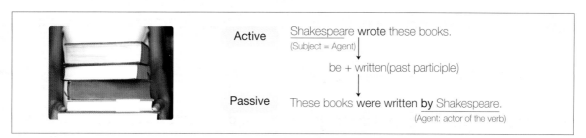

Active — Shakespeare **wrote** these books.
(Subject = Agent)

be + written(past participle)

Passive — These books **were written by** Shakespeare.
(Agent: actor of the verb)

- We also use the **passive** when we **do not know who does an action** or if it is **not important** or **necessary** to say who does something.

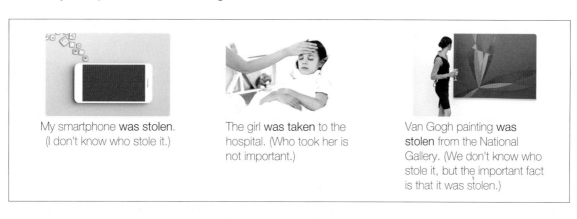

My smartphone **was stolen**.
(I don't know who stole it.)

The girl **was taken** to the hospital. (Who took her is not important.)

Van Gogh painting **was stolen** from the National Gallery. (We don't know who stole it, but the important fact is that it was stolen.)

- We form the passive with the **verb be** and the **past participle** (verb + -ed) of the main verb.

	Subject	Be	Verb+ -ed	by	Object(Agent)
Present Tense Passive	I	am			them. / her. / Tom.
	He, She, It, Thing	is	loved	by	
	You, We, They, Things	are			
Past Tense Passive	I, He, She, It, Thing	was	loved	by	them. / her. / Tom.
	You, We, They, Things	were			

69

Super Speaking in Grammar

A. Listen to the conversation and practice with a partner. Use the cues given. Then change roles and practice again. ⊙ Track 76

invent / the light bulb / ?
⇨ Thomas Edison

> Who **invented the light bulb?**
>
> The light bulb was invented by **Thomas Edison.**

invent / Hangeul / ?
⇨ King Sejong

design / the Eiffel Tower / ?
⇨ Gustave Eiffel

invent / the tea bag / ?
⇨ Thomas Sullivan

B. Work with a partner. Some people are telling lies. Read what they say, then use the words in brackets to correct the false statements.

That house was built by Eric.

No, It wasn't built by Eric. It was built by Jason.

Your turn now!

1. Eric   built that house.

   No ⇨ (Jason)

2. Sam   found the lost puppy yesterday.

   No ⇨ (Ava)

3. Kevin   drew the painting.

   No ⇨ (Jenny)

4. Nancy   created Snoopy.

   No ⇨ (Charles Schulz)

5. Bob   caught the thief last night.

   No ⇨ (the police)

6. Julie   invented the potato chips.

   No ⇨ (George Crum)

Unit 9 Invitations

Read and listen to the conversation. Work in pairs. Practice the conversation. ⊙ Track 77

Would you like to come to my party on Friday, Sarah?

Yes, I'd love to. Thanks, Richard!

How about you, Joseph? Can you come to my party?

Sorry, I can't. I have to finish my school project.

❋ What are you going to do this afternoon?   ❋ What do you usually do on your birthday?

❋ What do you say if you want to invite your friends to come to your (birthday) party?

A. Look at the pictures below. Then match the correct sentences to each picture.

1.  ☐

2.  ☐

3.  ☐

4.  ☐

a. I'm meeting a friend for lunch.   b. I have to baby-sit.

c. I have soccer practice.   d. I have a doctor's appointment.

71

Real Invitations

In Britain, people often invite friends for a meal, a party or just coffee. People who know each other very well may visit each other's houses without an invitation, but if we invite new friends, usually an invitation is needed. When people invite someone to their homes, they often say, "Would you like to come for dinner on Saturday?" Answers are, "Thanks, we'd love to. What time?" or "I'm sorry, We'd love to, but we're going to a concert." However, it is not polite to say, "No, we wouldn't."

Sometimes, the British use expressions that sound like invitations but which are not invitations. For example. "You must come over for a drink sometime." or "Let's go out for a meal one of these days." These are usually just polite ways of ending a talk. They are not real invitations because they don't mention an exact time or day. They just show that the person is trying to be friendly and the answers are, "Yes, that would be nice." or "OK, yes, thanks."

So next time you hear what sounds like an invitation, listen carefully. Is it a real invitation or is the person just being friendly?

meal

polite

carefully

A. Read and choose the correct answers.

Dear Nicola

It's Grandmother's 99th birthday on Saturday and everyone is here for the party. There are 15 people staying at our house this weekend. It's great to see everyone but our house is very crowded. My Aunt Doreen and Uncle Joe and their two children have my bedroom. Another aunt and her husband are sleeping in the living room. My brother has a bed in the dining room. And me? I'm sleeping in a tent in the yard!

See you soon,

George

1. Who has a birthday this week?

a. George   b. Aunt Doreen   c. George's grandmother

2. Where is George sleeping?

a. in his bedroom   b. in the yard   c. in the living room

3. Who's sleeping in the dining room?

a. George's brother   b. George's uncle and aunt   c. George's grandmother

B. Listen to the conversations and answer the questions. (⊙) Track 79

1. When will they have lunch together?

a. Friday

b. Thursday

c. Today

d. Tomorrow

2. What will the woman do tonight?

a. go to see a movie with the man

b. go to dinner with the man

c. go to the movie theater with her sister

d. go to the movie theater with the man

Dialog Track 80

Two students:

- Listen to the dialog and fill in the blanks.
- Listen again and check your answers.
- Read it together (change roles).

Ava	David ... David!
David	Yes? Oh, hi, Ava
Ava	_____ this evening?
David	I'm not sure. I'll probably stay at home. Why? _____?
Ava	I'm going to a soccer match, if _____.
David	Yes, sounds good. What time does it start?
Ava	_____ at the sports center.
David	OK. Is anyone from school going?
Ava	No, but someone you like _____.
David	Who?
Ava	Kathy!
David	Oh, OK. Shall I meet you outside the sports center at _____?
Ava	Yeah, OK, I'll see you there.
David	See you later, Ava.

● Discuss the questions below with your classmates.

1. If you could cook anything for dinner tonight, ...
  ▷ What would you cook? Why?
  ▷ Tell everyone about your ideas.

2. What is the first birthday you can remember?
  ▷ What happened?
  ▷ Can you tell everyone about it?

3. What happens when people are 60 years old in Korea?
  ▷ What is this birthday called?
  ▷ Tell everyone about it.

4. Traditionally, who asks for the recipient to attend the wedding on the invitations?

5. Do you send birthday cards to your family and friends?
  Yes! Why?
  No! Why not?

6. Do you send Teacher's Day or Parents' Day cards?
  Yes! Why?
  No! Why not?

7. Have you ever sent e-cards?
  Yes! How often? Who do you send them to?
  What is your favorite e-card site?
  Tell everyone about your e-cards.
  No! Why not? Do you want to?

Super Speaking!

A. Listen to the conversation and practice with a partner. Use the cues given. Then change roles and practice again. Track 82

go camping / this weekend /?
⇨ have to / finish my homework

> Would you like to **go camping this weekend**?
>
> I'd really like to, but I **have to finish my homework**.

see a movie / on Tuesday night / ?
⇨ have to / ask my mom first

join us / for dinner / ?
⇨ have a project / to do today

go skiing / this weekend / ?
⇨ be going to / a concert

B. Fill in your schedule for the weekend with six activities. Use the activities in the box or your own ideas. Ask and answer questions with a partner to find a time when you can meet. Remember to use *I'm*, *I have*, and *I have to*.

My Schedule		
FRIDAY	morning	
	afternoon	
	night	
SATURDAY	morning	
	afternoon	
	night	
SUNDAY	morning	
	afternoon	
	night	

baby-sit my brother   practice the cello

see a dentist's appointment   studying for a test

finish my homework   go to a party

practice soccer   go skiing

go skating   go fishing

A: Would you like to meet on Saturday morning?

B: Sorry, I have to practice the piano. Can you meet me later?

A: Sorry, I can't. I have to ...

Learn & Practice

- We use *let's* + base verb to make a **suggestion** for two or more people. *Let's* includes the **speaker**.
- *Let's* is a contraction of *let* + *us*, but we usually say and write *let's*.
- The negative form is *let's not* + base verb.

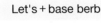

Let's + base berb	Let's + not + base berb

A: The movie theater isn't far away. B: Great! **Let's walk!**	A: Gasoline is too expensive. B: **Let's not go** by car.

- We use *would you like* ...? to **offer** things.
- We use *would you like to* ...? for **invitations**.

A: **Would you like** some cheese on your pasta? B: No, thank you.	A: **Would you like to** have lunch with me on Saturday? B: Yes, I'd love to.

A. Match the answers with *let's* or *let's not* to the following statements.

1. It's beautiful day.   a. Let's buy her a present.

2. Next Monday is a holiday.   b. Let's go for a walk.

3. It's Kathy's birthday next week.   c. Let's watch a DVD instead.

4. The movie starts in a few minutes.   d. Let's not stay at home.

B. Answer these questions about yourself with either *Yes, I would./No, I wouldn't* or *Yes, I do. /No, I don't.*

1. Do you like to ski?

⇨ _Yes, I do./No, I don't._

2. Would you like to have coffee after work?

⇨ _____

3. Would you like to go fishing on Sunday?

⇨ _____

4. Do you like ice cream?

⇨ _____

5. Would you like to come to my party?

⇨ _____

6. Would you like to participate in a debate?

⇨ _____

Super Speaking in Grammar

A. Listen to the conversation and practice with a partner. Use the cues given. Then change roles and practice again. Track 83

soccer / not have a soccer ball
⇨ volleyball

 Let's play **soccer**.

 I **don't have a soccer ball**.

 Well, Let's play **volleyball**.

 That sounds good.

tennis / not have a tennis racket
⇨ basketball

volleyball / not have a volleyball
⇨ table tennis

Around Town

Read and listen to the conversation. Work in pairs. Practice the conversation. Track 84

> Excuse me. Where is the ice cream shop, please?

> Go straight and turn right at the corner. It's next to the supermarket.

What are the man and the woman looking for?　　Where is the ice cream shop?

 **A.** Look at the pictures below. Then match the correct words to each picture.

 ☐

 ☐

 ☐

 ☐

 ☐

 ☐

1. turn left/right	2. next to	3. go straight
4. cross the street	5. behind	6. between

Reading Track 85

My Perfect Neighborhood

I have lived in my perfect neighborhood for five years. The street is very quiet, so there's no traffic noise. Some people like a lot of noise and crowds, but I like my quiet street. My house is between a big park and a post office. On the weekend, I sometimes jog in the park with my dad. There is a big Emart not too far away. A grocery store is two blocks from my house. Across the street from the grocery store, there is a hair salon, a dry cleaner's and a bank.

Next to the bank, there is a bookstore where students can buy their textbooks. So, you see, my neighborhood has everything that I need. The only thing that isn't close is my school. In fact, I need about 10 minutes to walk to the bus stop. I need to take two buses to get to school.

neighborhood

traffic noise

crowd

amusement park

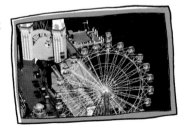

bakery

A. Look at the map below. Then listen and write the correct numbers. ⏺ Track 86

B. Look at the picture and complete the sentences.

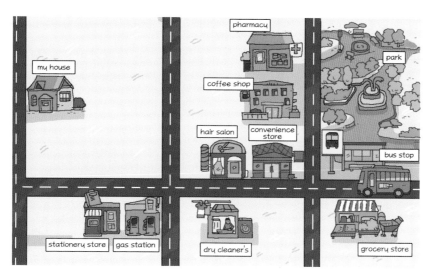

1. The hair salon is next to _the convenience store_ .

2. The dry cleaner's is across from _____ .

3. The coffee shop is between _____ and _____ .

4. The bus stop is in front of _____ .

5. The gas station is next to _____ .

Dialog   ● Track 87

Two students:

● Listen to the dialog and fill in the blanks.
● Listen again and check your answers.
● Read it together (change roles).

Cindy	Wow, this is such a big city! Look at the tall buildings!
Brian	Yes, I'm sure you'll love it here, Cindy.
Cindy	Is there any movie theater _____?
Brian	Yes, The movie theater in the city is _____.
Cindy	That's great. _____?
Brian	Go straight for two blocks and turn right at the corner. It's _____.
Cindy	Thanks. How long will it take?
Brian	It'll take _____.
Cindy	Is there a hanok village?
Brian	It's not far from here. _____. And then turn left at the corner. It's on your right. It's _____ the Hana Middle school.
Cindy	How long will it take?
Brian	It'll only take about 5 minutes. Last week, I visited the hanok village with my Korean friend, Suji. When we arrived at the village, I said, "Wow, did we take a time machine?" Suji said, "Yeah, we're in ancient Korean now." The village _____. Every house looked similar, but each one was _____.

● Discuss the questions below with your classmates.

1. Have you ever been on a subway train?

Yes! — Where? When? Tell everyone about it.

No! — Do you want to?

2. What was the best trip in your life?

▶ Why did you like it?

▶ Tell everyone about it.

3. Have you ever been to a hanok village?

Yes! — Where? When? Tell everyone about it.

No! — Do you want to?

4. What would you do if you had really noisy neighbors?

▷ Have you ever had a "dog problem" with neighbors?

5. If you could live anywhere in Korea, ...

▷ Which area would you choose?

▷ Why? Tell everyone about your choice.

6. What are the advantages and disadvantages of your neighborhood?

▷ What's the most interesting part of your home area?

7. What do the people in your community do for recreation?

Talk It Over

● What do you think of these ideas? Check(✓) your thoughts. Then talk with your classmates.

	Yes	No
1. Do you like to live far away from the city center?		
2. There are more accidents, because people become frustrated or angry due to the traffic jams.		

Super Speaking!

A. Listen and repeat the dialog. Then use the speaking cards to practice it with your partner.

Track 89

A: Excuse me. I'm looking for the ❶ ___restaurant___
   on this map.
   Could you help me? How do I get there?
B: Yes. Go straight for ❷ ___two blocks___ and
   ❸ ___turn right___. It's ❹ ___next to the park___.
A: How long does it take from here?
B: It takes about ❺ ___10 minutes___ on foot.
A: Great. Thank you for your help.

★You are here.

<movie theater>

❶ movie theater
❷ one block
❸ turn right
❹ next to the bank
❺ 5 minutes

<bookstore>

❶ bookstore
❷ three blocks
❸ turn left
❹ across from the library
❺ 15 minutes

<bakery>

❶ bakery
❷ two blocks
❸ turn left
❹ in front of the library
❺ 10 minutes

<post office>

❶ post office
❷ three blocks
❸ turn right
❹ next to the school
❺ 15 minutes

Learn & Practice

- We use **prepositions of place** to say where somebody or something is.

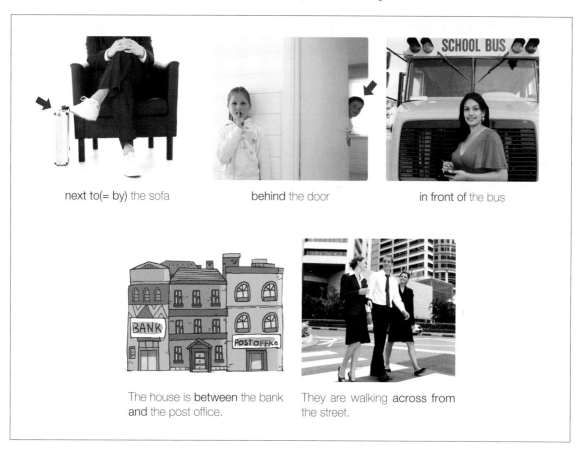

next to(= by) the sofa

behind the door

in front of the bus

The house is **between** the bank and the post office.

They are walking **across from** the street.

A. Using the map, complete each sentences with the name of a place.

1. The school is next to _____the bank_____.

2. The KFC is next to _____.

3. _____ is between the shoe shop and the post office.

4. The restaurant is across from _____.

5. The record shop is between _____ and _____.

school	bank		flower shop
	KFC		
hospital	record shop		shoe shop
	bookstore		restaurant
			post office

Super Speaking in Grammar

A. Listen to the conversation and practice with a partner. Use the cues given. Then change roles and practice again. Track 90

a woman / behind / the bookcase / ?
No ⇨ she / in front of

Is there **a woman behind the bookcase?**

No, **she is in front of** the bookcase.

a man / next to / the door / ?
No ⇨ he / behind

a bank / in front of / the post office / ?
No ⇨ it / between the post office and the restaurant

a school / behind / the park / ?
No ⇨ it / across from

B. Work with a partner. Look at the map below. Your partner must guess where you are.

I'm looking for you.
Where are you now?

It's next to the coffee shop.

You're at the pharmacy.

Right! Your turn now!

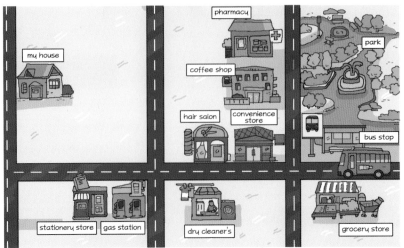

Unit 11

On Vacation!

Read and listen to the conversation. Work in pairs. Practice the conversation. (●) Track 91

Cindy, did you have a good time last vacation?

Yes, I did. It was wonderful.

Where did you go on vacation?

I went to Jeju-do to see my grandparents.

※ Where did Cindy go last vacation?   ※ Did she really have a good time there?

※ Where did you go on summer/winter vacation?

A. Look at the pictures below. Then match the corret phrases to each picture.

 ☐

 ☐

 ☐

 ☐

 ☐

1. go to Jirisan with my family
2. visit my grandparents
3. go to the beach
4. go camping with my family
5. go on a bicycle trip to Gangwon-do

87

Reading   Track 92

My Summer Vacation!

Hello! My name is Tiffany. I'm 12 years old and I live in Seoul, Korea. How was your summer vacation? Did you have fun? My best vacation was last summer vacation. It was fantastic for me. My parents took my younger brother and me to Paris last August. We went there by airplane. We stayed for five days in a small hotel in the city center. The hotel was not cheap, but it was not expensive. Our room was OK - it was old and dark, but very clean. In the mornings, we visited all the famous tourist sights and the most famous museums. The Louvre Museum was my favorite! I saw one of the most famous pictures in the world. It is called "Mona Lisa" by Leonardo Da Vinci. I was so impressed. We had sandwiches for lunch in a park. In the afternoon, we walked around the city. We took a lot of photos! It was so exciting! Three days we had crepes! They're delicious After a

nap and a shower, in the evenings, we had dinner in small restaurants and then we went for a walk. We visited interesting places and we met very interesting people! We also made some good friends. We didn't buy any presents. Everything was very expensive. But My younger brother and I sent very beautiful postcards to our friends. We had a very good time. It was a fantastic vacation!

A. Write the correct words under each picture. Use the words from the box.

postcard   crepe   parents   take photos   clean   exciting

1.

_____

2.

_____

3.

_____

4.

_____

5.

_____

6.

_____

Super Activity!

A. Listen and number the correct pictures. Track 93

1.

2.

3.

4.

Dialog ⊙ Track 94

Two students:

● Listen to the dialog and fill in the blanks.
● Listen again and check your answers.
● Read it together (change roles).

Suji	What _____ this summer vacation, Eric?
Eric	I had a big adventure with my father during my summer vacation. In the middle of summer, my father and I _____ to Gangwon-do for three days.
Suji	Really? That sounds like a big challenge.
Eric	It was. We rode our bicycles all day and _____ at night. The weather was hot, and we had to go up and down a lot of hills.
Suji	Wow. _____?
Eric	It was not easy, but I rode slowly and looked around at the trees, the rivers, and the mountains. I could feel nature and _____. How was your summer vacation? _____?
Suji	I went to the amusement park with my cousins.
Eric	Really? That sounds really fun.
Suji	It was. We rode a roller coaster.
Eric	Wow. _____?
Suji	It was scary at first, but I really enjoyed riding it. We had a very wonderful time. It was an exciting vacation!

Pair Work Ask and answer the question about the dialog with your partner.

A: What did the boy do during the summer vacation?
B: He _____ to Gangwon-do for three days.

90

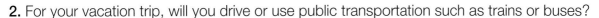

Super Discussion! ⊙ Track 95

● Discuss the questions below with your classmates.

1. Which do you think is the best season for a vacation?
> Explain why.
> Do you prefer summer or winter vacations? Why?

2. For your vacation trip, will you drive or use public transportation such as trains or buses?
> Explain to everyone.

3. Did you enjoy your last vacation?
> Why did you visit the place(s) you went to?
> How did you get there?
> How long were you there?
> What did you do there?
> Explain to everyone.

4. Did you meet any interesting people?
> Can you tell everyone about them?

5. Did you study during the vacation? If so, what did you study?

6. Where do you want to go in the future for your dream vacation?
> Explain to everyone.

7. What was the most interesting thing that you did during the vacation?
> Explain to everyone.

Talk It Over

● What do you think of these ideas? Check(✓) your thoughts. Then talk with your classmates.

	Yes	No
1. Do you think summer vacation should be longer?		
2. Summer vacation can disturb some student's daily routines?		
3. Summer vacation is so important because it lets teenagers take a break from their everyday school life.		

91

Super Speaking!

A. Listen to the conversation and practice with a partner. Use the cues given. Then change roles and practice again. ⊙ Track **96**

⇨ go to the Great Wall

> Where did you go on vacation?
>
> I **went to the Great Wall**.

⇨ go hiking with my family

⇨ go to a summer camp

⇨ go to the beach with my classmates

B. Listen and repeat the dialog. Then use the speaking cards to practice it with your partner.

 ⊙ Track **97**

A: What did you do this summer?

B: I ❶ _went to the amusement park_ with ❷ _my friends_ .

A: Really? What did you do there?

B: We ❸ _rode a roller coaster_ . It was very exciting.

❶ went to the zoo
❷ my family
❸ saw tigers, lions, and monkeys

❶ went to the concert hall
❷ my older sister
❸ met our favorite movie star

Learn & **Practice**

- We often use *one of the* before a **superlative** form. The noun that follows is **plural**.

Seoul is **one of the biggest cities** in the world.

Yellow dust is **one of the most serious problems** in Korea.

- To form a **gerund**, we add *-ing* to the base form of the verb. Like a noun or a pronoun, the gerund can be **the subject** or **the object** of a sentence. When we use a gerund as the subject, the gerund **subject** takes a **singular verb**.
- After certain verbs, we only use a **gerund** as the **object**.

Jogging every day **is** good for your health.
Nancy enjoys **jogging** in the morning.

Verb		Object
enjoy finish give up keep mind avoid + stop put off quit dislike		verb + -ing

A. Complete the sentences as in the example. Using *one of + the* superlative form.

1. Cristiano Ronaldo is ___one of the richest athletes___ (rich athlete) in the world.

2. The Beatles were _____ (successful rock band) in the world.

3. Mt. Mckinley is _____ (high mountain) in the world.

4. Yuna Kim was _____ (attractive athlete) in the world.

B. Make sentences using the prompts as in the example. Use a gerund.

1.

Jane / enjoy / eat healthy food

⇨ _Jane enjoys eating healthy food._

2.

Kathy / avoid / fight with her sister

⇨ _____

3.

Karen / finished / do her homework

⇨ _____

4.

speak in English / is hard at first

⇨ _____

Super Speaking in Grammar

A. Listen to the conversation and practice with a partner. Use the cues given. Then change roles and practice again. ⊙ Track 98

big problem / in the world / ?
⇨ hunger

 In your opinion, what is **one of the biggest problems in the world.**

 I think **hunger is one of the biggest problems in the world.**

big city / in Asia / ?
⇨ Tokyo

famous landmark / in Korea / ?
⇨ the Seoul Tower

beautiful place / in the world / ?
⇨ Venice

Getting Ready

Read and listen to the conversation. Work in pairs.
Practice the conversation. ⊙ Track 99

> What do you think of TV, Jane?

> I think TV is fun. Nancy, do you think TV is fun, too?

> No, I don't think so. I think TV is bad for children. A lot of programs are too violent.

※ Who thinks TV is bad?

Why does Jane think TV is good?

※ What do you think of TV? Why do you think so?

A. Look at the pictures below. Then match the correct phrases to each picture.

1. too violence in TV programs
2. get much knowledge by watching TV
3. tend to eat more junk food while watching TV
4. have many interesting functions
5. my favorite mini-series actor

95

Reading Track 100

The Influence of Television

Television has changed people's lives much since it was invented. Now it has become one important part of modern life. Television gives many benefits to us. For example, by watching TV, we can have a further understanding of the social situation and the culture of different countries. Moreover, television can provide people with much entertainment for the common people. We can enjoy ourselves very much while watching TV; it helps us forget our problems, at least for a short moment. We can communicate with many other people through television. We also get information, we get much knowledge by watching TV, and we learn fast in this way because this is always interesting. However, just as every coin has two sides, television has both advantages and disadvantages. Television has created some serious problems as well. Some people spend a lot of time watching TV every day. Watching too much TV is bad for your eyes. Moreover, watching TV is bad for our health because we tend to eat more junk food while watching TV. People no longer have enough time for hobbies, entertaining activities, and other outside amusement like theaters, sports. etc. Television prevents people from communicating with each other. Especially, Television has great negative influence on children. There are too much violence in TV programs. This is having a really negative influence on children's behaviors. Besides, they become lazy instead of going out.

They cannot live without television. So, we must try to find out some ways to solve the problems. Therefore, parents should avoid harmful programs, and limit the time they spend watching TV.

A. Write the correct words under each picture. Use the words from the box.

| avoid | communicate | invent | entertainment | violence | knowledge |

1.

_____

2.

_____

3.

_____

4.

_____

5.

_____

6.

_____

Super Activity!

A. Listen and number the correct pictures. ⊙ Track 101

1.

☐

2.

☐

3.

☐

4.

☐

Dialog · Track 102

Two students:
- Listen to the dialog and fill in the blanks.
- Listen again and check your answers.
- Read it together (change roles).

Grace	_____ do you like?
Eric	I like watching a reality show. It's my favorite.
	What do you think of today's TV programs?
Grace	Well, they are terrible. Most programs are a complete _____.
Eric	Do you think so? I _____. Some programs are very good.
Grace	Did you buy a new smartphone?
Eric	Yes, I used an old phone but all my friends were using smartphones. I couldn't use the free text messaging app, so I bought a new smartphone.
Grace	It looks really nice!
Eric	Thanks, but I'm not happy with it.
Grace	Why? Can you tell me _____? It must have many interesting functions.
Eric	It does, but a better one came out soon after I bought it.
Grace	Don't be too disappointed! The new model has _____ as yours.
Eric	Even so, the new model seems _____.

● Discuss the questions below with your classmates.

1. What kind of TV programs do you like to watch?
> ▶ Why do you like it?
> ▶ When is it on? Does your father like it, too?

2. TV commercials: useful or a waste of time?
> ▶ What do you think?

3. Do you ever watch a mini-series on TV?
> **Yes!** Which mini-series do you watch?
> Why do you like it?
> Why are TV mini-series so popular?
> **No!** Why not?

4. Is watching TV good or bad for you?
> ▶ Explain your opinion.
> ▶ Could you live without television? Explain your opinion.

5. Why are Korean dramas popular abroad?
> ▶ Why are they popular in Japan and China?
> ▶ Why are Korean actors popular in other countries?
> ▶ Explain your opinion.

6. Who is your favorite mini-series actor?
> ▶ Why do you like him or her?
> ▶ Tell everybody about your opinion.

7. Do you ever watch reality TV shows?
> **Yes!** Why? What do you like about it? Tell everyone your opinions.
> **No!** Why not? Tell everyone your reasons.

8. What are the advantages/disadvantages of watching TV?

Super Speaking!

A. Listen to the conversation and practice with a partner. Use the cues given. Then change roles and practice again. ⊙ Track 104

good
⇨ is exciting

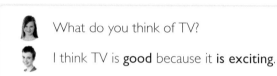

What do you think of TV?

I think TV is **good** because it **is exciting**.

good
⇨ is useful

bad
⇨ is too violent

bad
⇨ makes me lazy

B. Listen and repeat the dialog. Then use the speaking cards to practice it with your partner.

⊙ Track 105

A: Did you watch TV yesterday?

B: Yes, I watched ❶ _the news_ before ❷ _going to_ _____ bed bed last niight _____.

A: Do you like watching TV.

B: No, not much. But it gives me something to do when I'm bored.

A: What's your favorite TV program?

B: I enjoy watching ❸ _Korean soap opera_ the most.

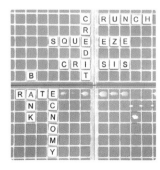

❶ the quiz show

❷ having a bath

❸ reality shows

❶ the documentary

❷ having dinner

❸ sitcoms

Learn & Practice

- We use the conjunction *because* to give a **reason** for something or to say **why something happens**. *Because* answers the questions *why*.

- We use the conjunction *so* to join two sentences. *So* gives us the **result** of an action or thought. We must use a **comma** before *so*.

It started to rain, **so** she opened her umbrella.

She was very upset **because** he didn't remember her birthday.

- We use the form of *have(has)* + **past participle** for the present perfect.

- We use the **present perfect** for an action or situation that happened at some unspecified time in the past. The exact time is not mentioned because it is not important. We put more emphasis on the action.

Cindy **has bought** a new car.
(When did she buy it? We don't mention the exact time because it isn't important. What is important is the fact that she's got a new car.)

- We use the **present perfect** for an action that started in the past and is **still continuing** in the present.

Tiffany **has been** a nurse since 1999.
She **has worked** in the hospital for 20 years.
(She started working as a nurse in 1999 and she still is a nurse.)

- We use the **present perfect** for an action that **has recently finished** and its result is visible in the present.

They **had finished** their shopping.
(We can see that they have finished their shopping because they're leaving the supermarket and there are bags in their shopping cart.)

A. Make sentences in the present perfect tense.

> live on the farm all his life   eat at that restaurant many times
>
> ride a horse before   be a teacher since 2010

1.

Steve _has lived on the farm all his life_ .

2.

Nancy _____.

3.

They _____.

4.

Kathy _____.

B. Complete the sentences with *so* or *because*.

1. I'm very hungry ____because____ I didn't eat anything today.

2. The weather was wonderful yesterday, _____ we went to the park.

3. My dad couldn't watch the news yesterday _____ the TV was broken.

4. The movie was very long, _____ we got home late.

Super Speaking in Grammar

A. Listen to the conversation and practice with a partner. Use the cues given. Then change roles and practice again. Track 106

❶

Steve / fail / the test / ?
⇨ he / not study

 Why did **Steve fail the test?**

He failed the test because **he didn't study.**

❷

the girls / laugh hard / ?
⇨ the joke / is very funny

❸

Jane's family / have / problems / ?
⇨ Her father / lose his job

First Step in

English Discussion

2

Answers

Unit 01 At Home

Getting Ready

A. 4 – 2 – 8 – 1 – 6 – 3 – 5 – 7

Reading

Victoria Beckham, two bathrooms and three bedrooms

Building Vocabulary

A. 1. build   2. pop group   3. wedding reception
   4. terrace   5. charity   6. two floors

Super Activity!

A. 1. On top of the TV   2. In the bookcase
B. 1. No, it isn't.   2. Yes, they are.

Dialog

live in a house, How many rooms, each floor, on the
second floor, seem to like, fun, never dreamed of, one
small problem, Are you trying to, where

Answer the Questions

1. F   2. F   3. T   4. F

Language Focus!

A. 1. on   2. in   3. in   4. on   5. on/under   6. on
B. 2. Are there, there are   3. Is there, there isn't
   4. is there, there isn't   5. are there, There are

Unit 02 Past Events

Getting Ready

A. 3 – 6 – 4 – 2 – 5 – 7 – 8 – 1

Super Activity!

A. 1. b   2. a
B. 1. 3   2. 1   3. 2
C. 1. F   2. F   3. F   4. T

Dialog

weekend, Nothing special, watched, Why not, so boring,
What did you do, cleaned my room, did my homework, a
blind date, chemistry

Unit 03 Describing People

Super Activity!

A. 1. a   2. b
B.

	is ...	has ...	wearing ...
Cindy	tall, heavy	curly brown hair	a red shirt and a blue blouse
Kelly	short	short blond hair	jeans and a white shirt

Dialog

health club, in great shape, regularly, headband, wearing,
blond hair, black curly hair, average height, well-dressed,
By the way, moustache

Language Focus!

A. 2. Why are they hungry?   3. How is the food?
   4. When is the concert?
   5. Why were you late yesterday?
   6. Where is the station?

Unit 04 Hobbies

Getting Ready

A. 7 – 4 – 2 – 5 – 3 – 8 – 6 – 1

Building Vocabulary

A. 1. rugby   2. musician   3. singer   4. cycling
   5. skateboarding   6. dancing

Super Activity!

A. 1. 2   2. 3   3. 1
B. 1. b   2. a   3. a

Dialog

favorite animation, Why do you like it, in your free time, go
inline skating, want to go, would you like to join, Where do
you want, the parking lot, by 10:00

Answer the Questions

1. F   2. F   3. T   4. F

Language Focus!

A. 1. to take   2. to meet   3. to drive/driving   4. to watch
   5. to study   6. to sing/singing

Unit 05 Movies

Getting Ready
A. 1. action movie   2. comedy   3. animated movie
   4. science fiction   5. horror   6. romance

Building Vocabulary
A. teenagers – 2, character – 5, sorcerer – 6, sell – 4,
   writer – 1, translate – 3

Super Activity!
A. 1. 2   2. 3   3. 1
C. b

Dialog
a reporter, Why not, Do you go to movies, every Saturday,
science-fiction movies, interesting and exciting, horror
movies, animated movies, really boring, Here are two free
tickets

Language Focus!
A. 2. have been   3. has finished   4. has rained
   5. have eaten   6. has given up
B. 1. for   2. since   3. since   4. for

Unit 06 Weather

Getting Ready
A. 1. cold and snowy   2. hot and humid
   3. wind and rainy   4. cool and sunny
   5. warm and cloudy

Building Vocabulary
A. 1. spring   2. winter   3. children   4. wake up   5. field
   6. holiday

Super Activity!
A. 1. 3   2. 1   3. 4   4. 2
B. Stay inside – Louis, Steven
   Go outside – Jennifer, Gregory

Dialog
How's your trip, weather is perfect, Did you see, on the
news last night, hit the city, people were hurt, I can't
believe it, have stopped, warm and sunny

Unit 07 Summer Plans

Getting Ready
A. 6 – 5 – 2 – 7 – 1 – 4 – 3 – 8

Building Vocabulary
A. 1. housework   2. trip   3. leave   4. plan   5. take walks
   6. cabin

Super Activity!
A. 1. 3   1. 1   3. 2
B. Patrick – b, Wendy – c, Scott – a

Dialog
any special plans, What do you do there, swimming and
boating, soccer or badminton, tell scary stories, What are
you doing this summer, is going to get married, When are
you going to leave, for six days, an interesting country

Pair Work
1. go camp with his family
2. go swimming, boating, play soccer, badminton, sit
   around a campfire, scary stores
3. is going to get married there

Language Focus!
A. 2. My father and I are flying to tokyo.
   3. My sister is meeting us there.

Unit 08 Transportation

Getting Ready
A. 2. b   3. c   4. a   5. f   6. d

Building Vocabulary
1. subway   2. convenience   3. transportation
4. entrance   5. crowed   6. backpack

Super Activity!
A. 1. b   2. b   3. a
B. 1. one kilometer   2. two kilometers   3. ten kilometers

Dialog
do I need, This is my first visit, how to ride, to your destination,
how often do the trains come, every six minutes, written in
English, it is a ten-minute walk, can also take a yellow,
drop you off at the bus stop, where you got off

Unit 09 Invitations

Getting Ready
A. 1. b 2. c 3. d 4. a

Super Activity!
A. 1. c 2. b 3. a
B. 1. b 2. c

Dialog
Are you doing anything, What are you up to, you're interested, It's on at nine o'clock, is going to be there, about eight thirty

Language Focus!
A. 2. d 3. a 4. c
B. 2. Yes, I would. / No, I wouldn't.
   3. Yes, I would. / No, I wouldn't.
   4. Yes, I do. / No, I don't.
   5. Yes, I would. / No, I wouldn't.
   6. Yes, I would. / No, I wouldn't.

Unit 10 Around Town

Getting Ready
A. 3 – 4 – 1 – 5 – 6 – 2

Super Activity!
A. 5 – 4 – 2 – 1 – 3
B. 2. the grocery store 3. the pharmacy, the convenience store 4. the park 5. the stationery store

Dialog
near here, nearby, How do I get there, on your left, about 20 minutes, Go straight for one block, next to, was amazing, different

Language Focus!
A. 2. the record shop 3. The restaurant 4. the bookstore
   5. the KFC, the bookstore

Unit 11 On Vacation!

Getting Ready
A. 2 – 4 – 3 – 1 – 5

Building Vocabulary
A. 1. parents 2. clean 3. take photos 4. exciting
   5. crepe 6. postcard

Super Activity!
A. 1. 4 2. 3 3. 2 4. 1

Dialog
did you do, went on a bicycle trip, slept in a tent, How did you do it, enjoy riding, Did you have fun, How was it

Pair Work
went on a bicycle trip

Language Focus!
A. 2. one of the most successful rock bands
   3. one of the highest mountains
   4. one of the most attractive athletes
B. 2. Kathy avoids fighting with her sister.
   3. Karen finished doing her homework.
   4. Speaking in English is hard at first.

Unit 12 Smart Life

Getting Ready
A. 2 – 5 – 4 – 3 – 1

Building Vocabulary
A. 1. invent 2. entertainment 3. communicate
   4. knowledge 5. violence 6. avoid

Super Activity!
A. 1. 4 2. 3 3. 2 4. 1

Dialog
What kind of TV programs, waste of time, don't think they are that bad, what's wrong with it, almost the same functions, much better than mine

Language Focus!
A. 2. has been a teacher since 2010
   3. have eaten at that restaurant many times
   4. has ridden a horse before
B. 2. so 3. because 4. so

106